CHASTIE'S VAGABOND'S HOUSE

Santa Monica WELCOMES YOU

Close Cover Before Striking

PERINO'S RESTAURANT

OCOANUT GROVE

"The Host of the Coast"

SANTA MONICA ELKS
906
21ST & WILSHIRE BLVD.
SANTA MONICA, CALIF.
Phone EXbrook 5-9906

Roberts Bros. Sandwiches

"THE WILSHIRE" . . . Vermont Avenue at Wilshire

The BROWN DERBY

The Gaylord HOTEL
and APARTMENTS
3355 WILSHIRE • LOS ANGELES
A HARRIS OPERATED HOTEL
CLOSE • COVER • BEFORE • STRIKING

FOOD TO TAKE OU[T]
WU'S GARDEN CHINESE FOOD
CLOSE COVER FOR SAFETY

Southern California's Most Beautiful
Apartment Hotel

WESTWOOD MANOR HOTEL
10527 Wilshire Blvd.

NEVER CLOSES

Ship's Coffee Shops

BE SAFE—CLOSE COVER BEFORE STRIKING

WILSHIRE
BOULEVARD
Grand Concourse of Los Angeles

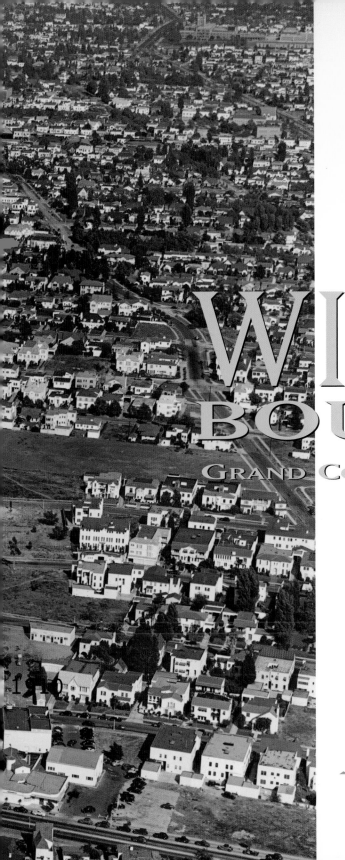

WILSHIRE BOULEVARD

GRAND CONCOURSE OF LOS ANGELES

KEVIN RODERICK

WITH RESEARCH BY

J. ERIC LYNXWILER

Introduction

BEFORE ANYONE CAN HOPE to decipher the maze-like geography of Los Angeles, it helps to know where Wilshire Boulevard fits in. For 15.8 miles it swoops through the sprawl, tying downtown to the Pacific Ocean along a promenade that, like the city itself, is an accidental creation of civic ambition and personal hubris. No one could have designed Wilshire Boulevard to assume such a commanding place in the story of modern Los Angeles.

It was assembled piecemeal while Los Angeles grew up from a dusty Mexican pueblo into the first metropolis to commit its future to the seductions and tempestuous double-crosses of the automobile. In a city with no real physical heart, old roads that went by the names of *El Camino Viejo*, Orange Street and Nevada Avenue were commandeered and used to invent an unofficial Main Street labeled Wilshire Boulevard. It's not the oldest, longest or most beautiful drive to spill across Los Angeles, but Wilshire is "an insinuating piece of the landscape that

Seen through trees lining Lafayette Park, the new Bullock's Wilshire department store towers above boulevard residences. Facing the park is the Town House apartment–hotel, which advertised itself as "Southern California's most distinguished address" when it opened in 1929.

8

The Art Commission's Unanimous Choice
For route of Archway
Worlds most beautiful drive

Proposed Archway *from* Westlake Park *via* Wilshire *and* San Vicente Boulevards *past* Brentwood Country Club Estates *to* Santa Monica Palisades.

no one can escape," in the words of architecture critic Harriette von Breton. Angelenos who appreciate Wilshire's importance never feel lost within sight of the mismatched skyline of Art Deco spires, multi-flavored office towers, million-dollar penthouses and soaring monuments splashed with Jazz Age neon.

Natives and tourists alike have been known to answer the call to explore the whole thing end to end, often in a convertible with the top down or on bicycles. Artist David Hockney pedaled the entire length on his second day in town. Others walk Wilshire and treat the quest like a pilgrimage, devoting a long day to the hike up and down more dips and inclines than passengers on four wheels realize.

Most who try begin downtown, where the boulevard appears, seemingly at random, between palm trees planted in front of the thirty-story One Wilshire building, which despite the name actually has a Grand Avenue address. This was not the original starting point. Grand Avenue has been the eastern

A 1922 real estate ad envisioned ceremonial arches soaring over Wilshire. They were a fanciful notion, but the boulevard did get widened and extended into downtown Los Angeles during the decade.

terminus only since the 1930s, when the most significant thoroughfare in Los Angeles finally reached downtown. Trekkers who make it all the way greet the Pacific between more palm trees, in front of a Depression-era statue of St. Monica on cliffs that soar above the beach. En route they traverse the hearts of two cities besides Los Angeles, cross a trio of telephone area codes, stroll over one interstate freeway and beneath another, and pass unaware over buried creeks.

The western passage encounters 206 cross streets that slice the boulevard into manageable corners and blocks, decorated with street art and architectural flourishes. Pedestrians notice urban phenomena that drivers miss—prehistoric goop oozing through the sidewalks near the La Brea Tar Pits, grinning monkeys sculpted into the wall of a 1920s art studio, feral cats roaming the abandoned Ambassador Hotel grounds. *National Geographic* magazine observed once that "virtually everything that has happened in Los Angeles has happened or is represented on Wilshire," and indeed it's a living museum of local history. The oldest surviving structure served as a chapel for Civil War volunteers. Eleven treasured buildings—including the soldiers' chapel—are listed on the National Register of Historic Places. Among those are the elegant Art Deco Bullock's

The Beaux Arts Talmadge apartments at Wilshire and Berendo added a touch of high-rise luxury. They were named for silent-film star Norma Talmadge, who lived briefly on the tenth floor with producer Joseph Schenk.

Wilshire department store and the refined Beverly Wilshire Hotel, built on the site of a 1920s racetrack. "Los Angeles looks like a city when you walk Wilshire," urban critic Art Seidenbaum wrote after one of his many crossings.

If you go, take a sweater. You can leave Grand Avenue in a summer heat wave and arrive at the ocean shivering in thick fog.

WILSHIRE BOULEVARD first appeared on maps in 1895 when a young manor-born real estate speculator cleared a swath across his barley field on the brushy western edge of town. Henry Gaylord Wilshire's dirt stripe went nowhere for four hundred yards, then lapsed in the weeds. Only later, after more entrepreneurial minds took over and motor cars arrived, did the boulevard expand to fulfill what urban historian Richard Longstreth calls its "leading role in Los Angeles's future."

As Los Angeles matured into a twentieth-century boom mega-city, Wilshire Boulevard evolved into an original creation—the first linear downtown, stretched out across the terrain like a string. The thousands of free spirits who tumbled into Los Angeles seeking a better life, converts from dirty Eastern cities and the Midwestern dust bowl, found the form appealing. They began to abandon the elaborate streetcar system which nourished the tightly compacted business section in the old center of town. They preferred driving their own Model Ts and Packards and living close to Wilshire's open spaces. A new idiom—the Wilshire district—crept into conversation.

Churches, department stores and other institutions left downtown to stake their future on the Champs-Elysees of the Pacific, which was how boosters hyped the creation. Mansions, hotels, movie palaces and nightclubs came too, accompanied by new grocery markets and more than one hundred gasoline stations. Parades and political protests were held on Wilshire Boulevard, where the adolescent city also learned how to use automated traffic signals

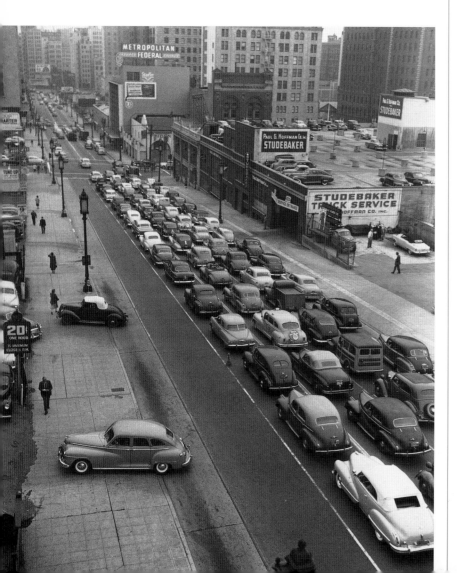

Wilshire Boulevard was designed to funnel traffic to and from the west side of the Automobile Age city. The left line of downtown-bound cars in this photograph clogs an experimental reversible lane.

and painted lane lines on blacktop. By the 1930s, historian Kevin Starr observed, "Wilshire Boulevard had become the central thoroughfare of the City of the Angels."

Its status as Grand Concourse of the Automobile Age city became fully certified when Charlie Chaplin and Buster Keaton frolicked along Wilshire in silent films, Raymond Chandler's hard-edged detective Philip Marlowe snarled the

Parking lots ruled even three decades after Wilshire reached Grand Avenue downtown. Architect Welton Becket's Standard Federal Savings, on the northwest corner, was called the "narrowest little skyscraper in the West" after its 1954 opening.

boulevard's name, and artists of distinction such as Hockney and Ed Ruscha interpreted its scenery on canvas. Wilshire Boulevard became a prestige address for Fortune 500 companies, a playground for movie stars at the Cocoanut Grove and Brown Derby, and a stopover for presidents and royalty. Cultural icon Marilyn Monroe is buried a few steps off the boulevard in Westwood, not far from the graves of more than eighty-five thousand American war veterans and their loved ones.

Over time, Wilshire Boulevard has relinquished some of its distinction to younger districts. High-rise offices, fashionable stores and the best restaurants and hotels can be found all over the city and in the suburbs. Yet the boulevard retains its stature as Main Street. It's an essential presence in the communities it passes through—Westlake, Wilshire Center, Koreatown, Park Mile, Miracle Mile, Beverly Hills, Holmby Hills, Westwood, West Los Angeles and Santa Monica. The boulevard reflects the immigrant

Wilshire Tower brought Art Deco excitement to the boulevard's Miracle Mile, still lined with vacant fields and oil wells in 1929. The rush to Wilshire was on. Traditional downtown men's store Desmond's took the east wing, Silverwoods the west.

mélange that is twenty-first-century Los Angeles. In churches once attended by mayors and judges, Sabbath services are held in a choice of languages. In Wilshire Center, once Los Angeles's prestige business address, the boulevard anchors the largest South Korean shopping community outside Asia.

The finest stores still aspire to be on Wilshire, and most foreign consulates in Los Angeles are located there. The boulevard functions as a media row for magazines, television producers and the entertainment industry, as well as the home of the Academy of Motion Picture Arts and Sciences. Living space along it is always in high demand.

Through the years, Wilshire has tried on many descriptive titles: first great processional of the Automobile Age, Fifth Avenue of the West, Grand American Avenue, Fabulous Boulevard. What it remains, without competition, is the Grand Concourse of Los Angeles. This is the story of Wilshire Boulevard.

The Ambassador Hotel reigned as the queen of Wilshire Boulevard's social swirl. Originally a country-style resort with horse stables, a zoo and pitch-and-putt golf, the hotel and its star-packed Cocoanut Grove nightclub came to define Wilshire glamour.

CHAPTER ONE

WILSHIRE'S TRACT

LOS ANGELES IN 1895 looked something like a young American city, but its soul still belonged to the past. Horses trotted through the dirt streets, pulling buckboards and tally-hos past slower-moving electrified trolley cars. Automobiles had yet to make an appearance. Pio Pico, the last Mexican governor of *Alta California* who could often be glimpsed sunning his ursine bones on the Old Plaza at the center of the former pueblo, had died only a year earlier.

One hundred thousand people already lived within the town limits. Most of them stayed close to the fickle stream that Pico knew as *Río Porciuncula*, which dripped out just enough water during the scorching summers to sustain a run of steelhead trout and keep the future of Los Angeles from evaporating

This earliest known photograph of the Wilshire Boulevard Tract was taken shortly after the subdivision was carved out of a barley field in 1895. Palm trees had just been planted in the parkway.

away. On maps, the dusty outer edge of town lay three miles west of the river, beyond the baked brown crest of Crown Hill, a rise covered in foxtails, oil wells and jackrabbit holes. Another fourteen miles farther toward the sunset, the cool blue Pacific Ocean beckoned. Escaping Los Angeles's desert heat for a pleasant afternoon at the beach required a wagon or steam train ride across a gently sloping plain cut by willow-lined creeks, past crumbling adobes and ranchos with romantic Spanish names like *Rodeo de las Aguas* and *San Jose de Buenos Ayres.*

"From Spring Street, west and as far as the coast, there was one huge field," nineteenth-century merchant Harris Newmark observed in his memoir. A rutted wagon trail dipped and bent through the wheat and barley stalks, snaking between rancho boundaries as far as the fuming tar pits where locals had collected sticky *brea* for longer than a century. *El Camino Viejo,* or The Old Road, had been carved by native Tongva feet and Spanish oxen hooves. It didn't look like much, but it was in the right place, pointing west toward the future.

Near the spot where the *camino* crossed the town limits, a flirtatious young rabble-rouser named Henry Gaylord Wilshire began in 1895 to clear a flat swath through his thirty-five acre barley field. On December 21, he filed subdivision papers announcing his plans to carve a magnificent wide boulevard, but the term was pure affectation. His creation would travel just twelve hundred feet, then expire in the brush. No one had any reason to suspect his boulevard, if that's what he called it, would someday connect with *El Camino Viejo* and other fragments of road to form Los Angeles's escape route out of the horse-drawn era.

That is what happened, of course. Wilshire's boulevard became the most important thoroughfare in the history of Los Angeles, his name forever etched across the face of the city. In his day, no one would have imagined that the Wilshire surname would come to stand for the ultimate in Los Angeles prestige and would still be spoken of highly more than one hundred years later. That would have sounded like folly among the Angelenos who knew of Gaylord Wilshire, which most inhabitants did.

He did not lack the wealth or personal accomplishments to name a boulevard after himself. Born into affluence on June 7, 1861, he grew up in Cincinnati across the street from a future president, William Howard Taft. Gay, as friends called Wilshire, attended Harvard for a year, toiled unhappily in the family banking and milling business, then in 1884 set out to help his brother William sell safes in San Francisco. For the rest of his life he traveled extensively, socialized at elite clubs and counted as longtime friends such well-known writers as George Bernard Shaw, H.G. Wells and Upton Sinclair, who once described Wilshire as "a small man with a black beard and a moustache trimmed to sharp points, and twinkling mischievous eyes—for all the world the incarnation of Mephistopheles." Admirers, and there were many, considered Gay Wilshire to be well-read and possessed of a keen wit and piercing intellect.

Others thought him to be a pompous fake. While he lived, Wilshire was snickered at for his voracious hunger to be in the spotlight. He ran for office in three countries and two states, always in defeat. At the slightest opening he erupted in public oratory, often accompanied by groans. He pursued numerous careers—grapefruit grower, gold miner, billboard mogul, inventor, publisher and real estate developer—but never met with unqualified success. Still, Gaylord Wilshire was not an easy man to dismiss, though the *Los Angeles Times* often tried, dubbing him a "flamboyant self-promoter." The rival *Express* derided him as a "social eccentric." When Wilshire died, a questionable final venture had earned him a reputation as "one of the really superb con men of his time."

At first, though, he fit comfortably into what passed for California society. He was blessed with wavy walnut-colored hair, smart taste in clothes and talented dancing feet. He wore a beard to hide a facial disfigurement picked up in a fall from a horse while scouting gold mines in the Sierra Nevada foothills, and he squired the daughters of moneyed families such as the Crockers. When a fare war between the Southern Pacific and Santa Fe railroads set off a transcontinental rush to the coastal plain around Los Angeles, the Wilshire boys headed south from San Francisco in 1886 to buy into the land boom. They were joined by their sister Clara and her husband, Charles C. Carpenter. With their father George's money, the Wilshires invested first in Long Beach, laying out an oceanfront subdivision and building a grand hotel. After it burned down, they relocated inland to what would soon be broken off from Los Angeles County and become Orange County.

Gaylord ran the Fullerton Land and Trust Company and, like many fortune-seeking new Californians, lost most of his land in the bust that followed the boom. For a while he grew walnuts and grapefruit and served as a bank officer. There remains a Wilshire Avenue in Fullerton and a Wilshire Square neighborhood in nearby Santa Ana. Los Angeles, though, was where he spent most of his time.

In Los Angeles, everyone who mattered in the 1880s and '90s probably knew the Wilshires. Society columns reported on their house parties and outings. Gaylord and William helped establish the California Club, the city's first private men's club. Other charter members included emerging leaders such as influential lawyer Henry W. O'Melveny, later a prominent booster of Wilshire Boulevard; banker Isaias Hellman, of another future Wilshire Boulevard family; and the ambitious developer of Venice-by-the-Sea, Abbot Kinney. Gaylord took up golf with relish when the game arrived in Southern California in 1897 and was invited to be a charter member of the Los Angeles Country Club. He also joined the Scribes, a select drinking club mostly of journalists and writers that met on Tuesday nights for four decades.

Gaylord's best move during the 1887 land boom had been to pay fifty-two thousand dollars for thirty-five acres of barley amid the weeds on the western town boundary. The wedge-shaped plot did not seem at first like a shrewd buy. Oil pumps belched on the parched, treeless hills nearby. Wilshire's investment held promise only due to its fortunate location in the path of Los Angeles's inevitable westward drift, on a lip of high land overlooking the town's rapidly blooming pride, Westlake Park. An expensive civic effort had transformed a swampy, alkali ravine into an oasis that the *Land of Sunshine*, a popular magazine, termed "the most popular open-air resort in the city . . . [with] fine drives, walks and flower beds." A year-round lake for boating and for entertaining the citizenry with floating July 4 fireworks made Westlake Park a glistening jewel.

Before Gaylord Wilshire could do anything with his lakeside barley patch, his life's path took a sharp detour. Like many Americans, he became

Henry Gaylord Wilshire, scion of a Cincinnati banking family, squandered several fortunes after arriving in California in 1884. Before his name came to personify Los Angeles prestige, many considered him a dilettante.

Westlake Park
"will gain much
in beauty after
the trees shall
have attained a
larger growth,"
the *Los Angeles
Times* enthused
in 1891.

enchanted with a utopian novel by Edward Bellamy, *Looking Backward: 2000–1887.* In the fantasy, an upper-class Bostonian falls asleep in 1887 and awakens at the millennium to find society transformed into a socialist nirvana. The novel "had more effect in converting Americans to socialism than any other single piece of literature," according to historian Thomas

S. Hines. Inspired readers formed political clubs all over the country to promote Bellamy's ideal. Gaylord Wilshire volunteered to be the movement's Southern California flag-bearer. In 1890, he became the first candidate to run for Congress as a Socialist. He lost, but embraced his new passion. His was Fabian socialism, more middle-class than revolutionary, and many

of his positions, such as women's suffrage and eight-hour workdays, would soon enter the mainstream.

After his father died, Gaylord inherited the financial means to pursue politics as a calling. He married Hannah Griffiths Owen, a wealthy Welsh woman, and adopted her daughter Norah. They left in 1890 for England, and en route Gaylord ran unsuccessfully for New York attorney general. For five years the Wilshires called London home. He gave passionate speeches in Hyde Park, lost an election for the House of Commons, and became a confidante of the Irish-born author and playwright George Bernard Shaw. Gaylord even grew a fuller Shavian beard, wore the same tweed suits as Shaw and assumed his colleague's florid oratory style.

Gaylord and Hannah divorced shortly after returning to Los Angeles in 1895. That was when he decided the time was right to make something of the barley field. William had moved back from San Francisco and become prominent in civic groups such as the chamber of commerce and La Fiesta, an

annual celebration of the city's Hispanic roots held partly in Westlake Park. William knew the governor and the top real estate agents in town, Gaylord knew how to sell a cause. They announced plans to become land developers.

Observers could be excused if they were skeptical of the brothers' Wilshire Boulevard Tract. It was remote from the center of town, located on the far, high side of Westlake Park. The tract's western border squeezed up against a muddy depression fouled by seeping *brea* and oil wells that the city called Sunset Park. This eyesore had been a gift to the people of Los Angeles from Clara Shatto, whose husband owned Santa Catalina Island and much of the Orange Heights section where Good Samaritan Hospital would be built. The other two sides of the Wilshire tract were formed by Sixth and Seventh streets, unpaved roads that led back into town.

New subdivisions around the periphery of Los Angeles were not unusual in the mid-1890s, but the Wilshires had grander ambitions. Across the

George and Clara Shatto built their magnificent residence on Orange Street, in the heights separating downtown and Westlake Park. The home received a Wilshire address when the boulevard was extended through the hills in the 1920s.

center of their land, they promised to grade a generous, one-hundred-twenty-foot-wide graveled boulevard. It would stretch just four blocks between the two parks, but the brothers believed that even a short stub of remarkable avenue would attract lot buyers. To spur sales, they lobbied to encircle the tract with special streetcar lines, but insisted that the city council forbid the laying of tracks—forever—on their boulevard. The brothers also offered a clever deal. The Wilshire company would build a second, intersecting boulevard beside Sunset Park if the city would provide the land. The council accepted, bless-

ing the fledgling tract with a confluence of two unusually wide promenades. There is some evidence that Gaylord initially wanted to name the park-to-park boulevard in honor of a relative on the Benton side of his family. Either out of dumb luck or some epiphany, it didn't happen. The broad cut connecting the parks was christened Wilshire Boulevard. The intersecting street on former city land became Benton Way. (After Sunset Park was renamed for the Marquis de Lafayette in 1918, Benton became South Lafayette Park Place.)

Perpendicular to their Wilshire Boulevard,

It required tons of fertilizer to transform Westlake Park's alkali soil into a refreshing splash of greenery on the city's dusty west side. Frolicking seals in the pond to the left of the path amused Sunday strollers.

Westlake Park, LOS ANGELES, Cal.   8541.

the brothers laid out four cross streets—Park View, Carondelet, Coronado and Rampart—with concrete curbs and sidewalks. Canary Island date palms were planted. These were costly improvements, but while Gaylord may have been a raving socialist, he possessed useful capitalist connections: financing came through Joseph A. Sartori, the head of Security Trust and Savings Bank and a fellow co-founder of the Los Angeles Country Club. The brothers talked up plans for a hundred-fifty-room tourist hotel on five acres at Park View and Seventh, overlooking the lake. But in tone the Wilshire Boulevard neighborhood was to be residential and exclusive, appealing to the upper strata of Los Angeles society. Gaylord himself lived for a time at 691 S. Carondelet Street.

Besides the ban on streetcar lines, the brothers got the city council to impose extra conditions that set Wilshire Boulevard apart. No hauling of coal, sand, manure or any heavy goods by "truck, dray, wagon, cart or other vehicle" was allowed. The mayor rejected a further gambit by the Wilshire brothers to have the city parks commission maintain the boulevard's trees, but the statement was made. Though the first motor car did not appear in Los Angeles for another two years, the restrictions encouraged Wilshire Boulevard's destiny as the showcase drive of the Automobile Age.

LATE IN HIS LIFE, Gaylord Wilshire claimed to be the genius behind the boulevard that bore his name. In truth, his role in the phenomenon never extended beyond the original tract. Developing real estate was not his forte. Instead, he became one of the most colorful eccentrics to inhabit the city's history.

While he was selling lots on Wilshire Boulevard, Gaylord was also pitching the notion of a perpetual motion machine and being reviled as the billboard king of Los Angeles. His favorite socialist slogan may have been "Let the nation own the trusts," but he made no apologies for holding a lucrative monopoly over outdoor advertising. Billboards were not beautiful, he conceded, but they were less offensive than "a badly designed building, a dirty street, a high death rate, a low birth rate, a weak novel or a moral coward," he wrote in a letter published in the *Times*. Wilshire papered his own subdivision and much of the city with advertising bills, and when leading real estate broker William May Garland objected, Gaylord quipped that "a man who wears a red necktie with an evening suit has no standing as an art critic." In 1900, though, a judge found Wilshire guilty of being a public nuisance for posting overly large billboards.

Later that year, he again ran unsuccessfully for Congress, but also won his only election ever—to a board of Los Angeles freeholders chosen to draw up a new city charter. Another member was Harrison Gray Otis, the irascible *Times* publisher whose paper had taken to calling Wilshire a faker and dilettante for spending so much time at the country club. His reply: "I like to play golf, but I like to make speeches better." Wilshire was soon in trouble again, this time for orating in downtown's Central Park, now called Pershing Square. The law he broke was a brazen effort to muzzle socialists, and he got off when an honest judge ruled the ordinance improper. The reprieve was brief. When a new law required a written permit for public speeches, Wilshire grabbed his Panama hat and made a show of being arrested. As officers led him away, he hollered that onlookers could read all the details in the latest Gaylord Wilshire venture, the *Challenge*.

Sailboats on the lake in Westlake Park, shown here in 1885, made a much better neighbor than the "thirty-five-acre mudhole" that Gaylord Wilshire found when he bought his adjacent barley field. He played an important role in improving the park.

His socialist newspaper debuted December 26, 1900, promising radical ideas and an optimistic point of view. The name was chosen to remind readers that Wilshire had offered ten thousand dollars to William Jennings Bryan if the Democratic Party candidate for president would debate him in public (Bryan never collected.) Wilshire soon demanded a bigger stage and in the fall of 1901 he moved the *Challenge* to New York City. He would not live in Los Angeles again for almost fifteen years, a time in which the city would actually come close to electing a socialist mayor, Job Harriman. In New York he upgraded the *Challenge* to a slick magazine and became embroiled in a dispute with the U.S. Post Office. After the 1901 assassination of President William J. McKinley, postal inspectors had clamped down on radicals and denied the *Challenge* the reduced postage available for periodicals. Faced with much higher mailing costs, Gaylord relocated the magazine to Toronto and gave the publication a more personal identity: *Wilshire's Magazine.* Canada became the third country in which he sought office.

By the time the magazine returned to Manhattan in 1904, *Wilshire's* had grown into an influential monthly of literary writing and political ideas. It published leading writers on the left such as Gaylord's friend Shaw, Leo Tolstoy and Jack London. Circulation reached four hundred twenty-five thousand, making Wilshire's "the most influential socialist journal in the United States," according to historian Kevin Starr. Wilshire hosted Russian Maxim Gorky on a controversial visit to New York and

helped win the right of tenants to withhold rent if their tenements lacked heat. Always up for a spirited debate, he made the papers in 1908 when he rose in the audience after an anti-Socialist play at the Savoy Theater and began, "If you don't mind I would like to say a few words . . . " Catcalls rained down as the orchestra drowned him out. Opponents thought him a windbag, but a letter to Wilshire from a reader in Lynn, Massachusetts, shows how widely his influence was felt. Beginning "Dear Comrade," the missive referred to enclosed photographs of a newborn baby named Gaylord Wilshire Gidney.

In New York, Wilshire also courted and wed a young artist and social worker from Illinois, Mary McReynolds. She wrote poetry for the magazine as "Godiva" and oversaw the women's department. Unlike his first wife, Mary shared Gaylord's political passion, made speeches and formed the Women's

National Progressive League. They were married February 6, 1904, with Julian Hawthorne, the son of author Nathaniel Hawthorne, serving as best man. R.H. Hay Chapman, managing editor of the *Los Angeles Herald,* dispatched the best wishes of Gaylord's old drinking buddies in Los Angeles: "I hope Mrs. Gay will be able to handle you. I admire her courage." They had a son, Logan, in 1906 and lived on both sides of the Atlantic. (Logan later wrote that his father had first married an Ailene Ivers, but he provided no details and no records have been found.)

Keeping the money-losing magazine afloat was a perpetual struggle. Wilshire was often closer to insolvency than his self-professed image as a millionaire socialist suggests. Dr. John Randolph Haynes, a political reformer who handled Wilshire's Los Angeles affairs and really was a millionaire socialist, traveled abroad with his friend and warned him often

Wilshire decorated his Manhattan magazine office with a bust of Tennyson and portraits of men he respected. On the day before his wedding to Mary McReynolds, he wrote her: "If you happen to be near St. Bartholomew's Church tomorrow about noon, you might look in and marry me . . . Don't bother if you have anything else to do."

Wilshire took jabs at political foes but also printed famous authors. Jack London's *People of the Abyss* debuted in the August 1903 issue, which was published in Toronto despite the New York address on the cover.

that the magazine was dragging him toward financial ruin. Haynes lent the magazine more than a hundred thousand dollars, writing in a letter, "Allow me to say, old man, that although I believe you are egotistical, by heavens, I think you have reason to be." Wilshire's mother made at least one loan then stopped answering his letters. Wilshire tried selling stock in the magazine to raise cash and dangled astonishing inducements in return for subscriptions, including new cars and a peach ranch in Ontario, California.

He never bothered to publicly disavow his image of substantial wealth. Upton Sinclair gave it credence in *The Jungle,* his 1906 novel exposing the sordid conditions in Chicago's cattle stockyards, when he alluded to a millionaire socialist whose magazine had been driven to Canada. Sinclair, who would later run for governor of California, credited Wilshire with his own conversion to socialism and explained that their enduring friendship was based on mutual succor: "For years we lived on the basis that when he had money he loaned it to me, and when I had it, I loaned it to him." There was nothing mutual, however, about the shocking appeal Sinclair made to "My Dear Mary and Gay" on June 28, 1909. Sinclair's utopian cooperative in New Jersey had burned to the ground, consuming most of his assets. He began by telling his friends they held in their hands "surely one of the most extraordinary letters that ever were written in this world." At the age of thirty, Sinclair counted himself a failure as a writer and blamed the ceaseless struggle to make money.

"I want to be free to do my work, and never have to think of money again; I would do anything in the world to be able to do this," Sinclair wrote. He proposed that the Wilshires guarantee him an annual allowance for life—plus a house near a university,

Mary, younger by twenty years, often took extended trips alone. "Dearest Lamb, I really don't seem to get as many letters from you as I should," Wilshire complained during a 1906 absence that included the birth in Florence of their son Logan. Gay and Mary are together here in England.

preferably on a coast, and enough funds to travel, see plays and educate his son. In exchange, Sinclair would devote all his writing talents to socialism and the Wilshires would own all rights to his work. "I am not joking," he assured his friends. "I want to put in several years on a big novel; and I don't want to have to wonder who will publish it if it fills three volumes."

Even if Gaylord had been inclined to sponsor Sinclair, he was in no position to do so. Socialists he had induced to invest in the Bishop Creek Gold Mine, a speculative venture in the eastern Sierras that failed to produce, were questioning his principles. His lack of revolutionary fire made Wilshire more suspect, and it didn't help that the federal government was investigating him and that the *New York World* took to calling him a "mining swindler." Gaylord and Mary left New York in 1910 for England, a self-imposed exile that only ended when World War I threatened and, once again, he came up short of money. In 1914 he made his way back to California to reestablish himself in Los Angeles.

Wilshire bought an eight-acre citrus ranch on Elizabeth Street in Pasadena and opened a downtown office on Hill Street. He also broke with socialism. The final issue of *Wilshire's* in 1915 called on the United States to enter the world war against Germany, and he urged vigilante attacks on antiwar socialists. In his fourteen-year absence from Los Angeles, much had changed. His original four-block Wilshire Boulevard had been paved most of the way from Westlake Park to the ocean. People drove Ford Model T's home to neighborhoods built where dairy cows roamed the last time he was in town. His sister Clara was still a society fixture, but William had returned to San Francisco, where he died in 1917.

Their half-brother Nathaniel, a popular golfing champion in the local clubs, had died in 1914. Gaylord, the inspiration of everything called Wilshire in modern Los Angeles, was at loose ends.

He golfed, wrote letters and attended gatherings of the Scribes. He marveled in letters to Shaw at the "irony of fate" that so many churches were located on the boulevard that bore the name of an atheist. Gaylord and Mary hosted salons in Pasadena that included literary and political figures, among them old writer friends such as Wells and Sinclair, a Pasadena neighbor. Mary had studied with Dr. Carl Jung in Switzerland and her growing practice as a psychoanalyst and interpreter of dreams—and author of several published books—brought in most of the household income. When Gaylord's stepmother Susan died in 1919, other family members received inheritances but Gaylord was left nothing. He later broke the will and got fifty thousand dollars, then poured the money into the Bishop gold mine, according to Logan.

Gaylord Wilshire tried in 1923 to get back into the flourishing Los Angeles real estate game. He set up offices at Wilshire Boulevard and Vermont Avenue and advertised for investors in a twelve-story office building he proposed to build. "Someday Los Angeles will be the premier city on this continent and Wilshire Boulevard the premier boulevard not only of Los Angeles but of the whole world," the pitches crowed. Every ad bore a likeness of Gaylord's now wildly-bearded face and his signature as the "originator of Wilshire Boulevard." He might have done better had the ads not also touted his belief that he had mystical powers as a financial prophet. No one rushed to do business with him. He received a gentle kiss-off in a letter from banker Marco Hellman, who sent along his good wishes: "It seems good to hear from one of the old timers, especially from one whose name is so closely connected with the Wilshire District. There are not many of them left now."

About the only encouragement evident in the Wilshire family archives at the University of California in Los Angeles is a note from the Kings Road studio of an Austrian-born architect of growing repute. He had seen the Wilshire real estate flyer and made his introduction:

> *Dear Mr. Wilshire,*
> *Will your vision be as keen architecturally as it was financially? I should like to plan your building—and give Los Angeles a glimpse into its architectural future.*
>
> *R.M. Schindler*

But there would be no Rudolf M. Schindler-designed buildings on Wilshire's boulevard, then or ever.

Gaylord closed the real estate office and considered selling vacuum cleaners. He was sixty-three years old, and Mary made a good enough living seeing clients that they had a weekend house among the movie stars on the beach at Santa Monica. Nevertheless, in 1925 he launched his most outlandish venture yet.

Wilshire marketed an electric device of his own invention, the I-On-A-Co electric belt, which he promoted as a cure for cancer, diabetes, tuberculosis and almost any other disease. He boasted of validation by research institutes and quoted amazing testimonials. "I-On-A-Co has stopped my hair from falling out and has now re-thatched my bald spot!" one ad claimed. In truth, the belt was a leather collar wrapped around eight pounds of meaningless wire coils that could be plugged into a wall socket. The doctors quoted in Wilshire's ads did not exist; the testimonials were from cronies. There was rich irony in Wilshire choosing this jag in his life's path. Twenty years earlier, *Wilshire's* had run ads for a book that chastised gullible socialists for falling prey to pitches by quacks, charlatans and "electric-belt men." Now Gaylord Wilshire was an electric-belt man.

The I-On-A-Co, however, was a commercial success. It sold for $58.50 each and in letters Wilshire boasted of shipping more than fifty thousand. The actual number may have been more. He apparently had no shame about pitching the belt to longtime friends. "People are completely transformed and the turning of the hair back to its original color is an almost everyday occurrence," he wrote to Shaw. Haynes, his physician friend and onetime brother in socialism, insisted that Wilshire never use his name in connection with the device. As questions mounted, the American Medical Association analyzed the belt and concluded, "As a cure for any physical ailment it is not worth five cents." Sales declined and legal action loomed.

The issue became moot on September 6, 1927, when Gaylord Wilshire passed away at age sixty-six in New York City. He suffered from inflammatory rheumatism and infectious arthritis, and died heavily in debt. Wilshire's passing merited a respectful but short obituary in the *New York Times* ("Former Magazine Editor and Mining Promoter") and was marked in the *Los Angeles Times* by five paragraphs that omitted mention of socialism. The funeral was small and unburdened by prominent mourners, with burial at Woodlawn Cemetery in the Bronx. It fell to *Los Angeles Saturday Night*, a weekly magazine edited by Samuel T. Clover, one of the Scribes, to give the life of Gaylord Wilshire more context:

I venture that no other person in Southern California had a larger acquaintance among those daring souls who depart the beaten track in pursuance of their ideals. Colorful, sanguine, widely read and traveled, his was a most interesting mind.

Gaylord Wilshire was a charming conversationalist, one of the few who made a study of the art of talking—and listening. No matter what the subject under discussion he always contributed to it a novel viewpoint or shed new light on it.

He lived every moment of his existence and his contact with other vivid minds made him always a most interesting companion. Peace to his restless soul!

Since his death, occasional suggestions have been made to strip Wilshire's name off the city's most important drive. The name Marine Boulevard was put forth in a fit of patriotism, and some historically minded person proposed Via Crespi to honor the priest who chronicled the first Spanish overland expedition through California. But they never got very far.

Before Logan Wilshire died in 1970, he prepared an unpublished manuscript that described his father as "too far ahead of the crowd to ever insert himself into the main stream of history." Wilshire senior probably would have agreed, since he often professed, without humility, to being on the leading edge with his vision of a wide boulevard heading toward the ocean from Westlake Park. "That it was destined to be the best part of Los Angeles was just as obvious to me then as it is to everybody now," Gaylord wrote in a 1924 real estate pitch. "It was very hard in 1896 to get people to agree with me."

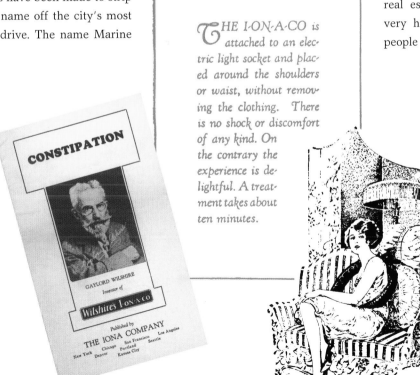

Wilshire's I-ON-A-CO

THE I-ON-A-CO is attached to an electric light socket and placed around the shoulders or waist, without removing the clothing. There is no shock or discomfort of any kind. On the contrary the experience is delightful. A treatment takes about ten minutes.

CONSTIPATION

GAYLORD WILSHIRE
Inventor of
Wilshire's I-ON-A-CO

Published by
THE IONA COMPANY
New York   Chicago   San Francisco   Los Angeles
          Denver   Portland   Seattle
                    Kansas City

The American Medical Association called Wilshire an "arch-quack" and his electric device a "magical horse collar." He assembled his I-On-A-Co belts at home in Pasadena and sold them through Owl drugstores.

In 1913, Sunset Park (later renamed Lafayette Park) had matured into a pleasant retreat. The street lining the park at the top left is Commonwealth Avenue. It intersects with Wilshire Boulevard just out of the picture at the far left.

CHAPTER TWO

BETWEEN THE PARKS

SOMEONE OF STATURE did believe in the boulevard's future, even if he didn't care for Wilshire the man. Harrison Gray Otis, publisher of the *Los Angeles Times*, detested socialists and billboards, and he clashed often with Gaylord Wilshire. That didn't stop Otis in 1898 from building an instant landmark on the most desirable corner lot on the new boulevard. The handsome two-story Mission Revival residence that he called the Bivouac enjoyed a perch overlooking Wilshire Boulevard's terminus at Park View Street. From his front portico, Otis could hear the slap of oars on the lake down a gentle slope in Westlake Park.

Architect John P. Krempel's Corinthian columns, ornamented chimneys and red-tile steeped

The **1898 Harrison Gray Otis mansion** at Wilshire and Park View Street gave the new boulevard a recognizable landmark. Even after he died and the Otis Art Institute moved in, postcards featured the former home as a Wilshire District icon.

roof, all set back from the boulevard at the top of a fine rising lawn, made a perfect advertisement. Indeed, the Otis home and its bountiful landscaping decorated postcards promoting Wilshire Boulevard and the Los Angeles way of life. But it was the presence of General Otis himself (he demanded the

honorific after receiving a commission in the Spanish-American War) that helped establish the new tract as a prestige address. He was a familiar sight around town in his white serge suits, felt hat and stringy beard. His confidence in Wilshire Boulevard conferred status, even among the many citizens of the city who loathed him.

A combative curmudgeon by nature, Otis had become editor and part owner of the *Times* in 1882, the year he arrived in Los Angeles from Ohio. Four years later he bought out his partner to become

Refrigerated-car inventor Edwin T. Earl built a brick home next door to General Otis, his publishing rival, on the boulevard's first block. Charles White Elementary School opened in 2004 on the site of both former landmarks.

sole owner. The *Times* parroted his views on foreign affairs, skewered his foes and advocated his vision of a vastly bigger and more Republican Los Angeles unbothered by labor unions. President Theodore Roosevelt called Otis an "enemy of every movement for social and economic betterment," but in Los Angeles what the general thought carried weight. He led the fight for the "free harbor" at San Pedro that dashed the Southern Pacific Railroad's plan to establish its own monopoly, Port Los Angeles, near Santa Monica. He played a crucial role in converting the San Fernando Valley from wheat fields to suburbs, and kept his own five-hundred-fifty-acre ranch in the valley chaparral. (It later belonged to *Tarzan* author Edgar Rice Burroughs, who dubbed the spread Tarzana.) One can surmise that Otis's influential presence may also have been the reason that dozens of teamsters were arrested and fined for violating the ban on hauling along Wilshire Boulevard.

His *Times* was no different from most of the papers sold on the streets of turn-of-the-century Los Angeles in pushing the publisher's agendas. On the first block of Wilshire Boulevard, however, perfect stasis prevailed. Otis's next-door neighbor was his opposite among local newspaper moguls. Edwin Tobias Earl had become rich after inventing the refrigerated railroad car that made it possible for Southern California citrus growers to ship fresh oranges and lemons to the East. After selling his fruit company, Earl bought the *Los Angeles Express,* the city's oldest paper, and steered it to be nearly as progressive as the *Times* was conservative. He aligned with leading reformers such as John Randolph Haynes, Gaylord Wilshire's friend and Otis's personal physician.

Otis at first included the Earls in social gatherings, including a gala reception at the Bivouac for President William J. McKinley, who slept overnight there during a 1901 visit. The publishers even invested together in a secret scheme to buy up arid San Fernando Valley ranch land in order to profit from the water that insiders knew would be flowing soon through William Mulholland's Owens Valley aqueduct. Over time, though, the rivalry between the publishers grew more vociferous and personal. The afternoon *Express* gleefully reported on Otis's arrest for brandishing a machete against a reporter for the *Herald*, the city's most Democratic paper. The morning *Times*, in turn, mocked E.T. Earl in headlines as *E. Toopious* and delighted in his indictment in a political influence investigation. After a grueling day of testimony, the *Times* headline gloated melodramatically, "Earl Writhes Under the Merciless Lash."

Earl's mansion at Wilshire Boulevard and Carondelet Street eschewed the Mission style that Otis favored and instead featured an English-style, ivy-covered brick design. British-born architect Ernest Coxhead, who relocated to Los Angeles in 1886, first designed the residence with wood shingles. Just before completion, however, a fire caused extensive damage. Starting over, Coxhead fashioned the home out of masonry, with a plethora of secret moving panels that fascinated visitors. It featured a beautiful oak stairway and fireplaces of cut stone trimmed in marble in every major room. Outside, tall evergreen trees and walking paths created a shady haven. Earl, who also started the *Los Angeles Tribune,* resided there until his death in 1919.

Similar affluent homes set an elite tone for the Wilshire district, a term that began to be heard as the twentieth century approached. Arthur Letts, founder of the Broadway department store, and retired Ohio entrepreneur Homer Laughlin, who built the city's first steel structure that houses the downtown Grand Central Market, bought home sites. On May 23, 1898, the first social notice in the *Times* to mention Wilshire Boulevard observed that "Judge and Mrs. C. N. Sterry entertained at dinner last evening at their residence on the Wilshire boulevard, in honor of Chief Justice Foster of Kansas." Gaylord Wilshire's hunch was proving out. Not only were leading citizens buying his lots, but Westlake Park, the tract's garden spot, was where the queen of the annual Fiesta de Los Angeles made her festive appearance to the citizenry, gliding across the lake in a decorative gondola. The prestigious Westlake School for Girls opened beside the park at Sixth and Alvarado streets. Owning a fine residence on Wilshire Boulevard became a status symbol, just as in Manhattan a mansion on Fifth Avenue testified to its occupants' elite station.

The true mark of Wilshire Boulevard distinction became a home designed by John C. Austin, another English-born architect who had come to Los Angeles in 1892, in his early twenties. During his later career, Austin would design such local landmarks as the Shrine Auditorium and Griffith Observatory and be part of the team that gave Los Angeles its iconic, pointed City Hall. Before those, he created the biggest and most talked about early buildings on the new boulevard. His work included a two-story Colonial Revival mansion for businessman

No single style dominated residential Wilshire, seen looking east toward Lafayette Park. Mansions were numerous but there also were neighborhoods of modest homes and high-rise apartments such as the Bryson, left, and the Arcady in the background.

Nicholas E. Rice at 2520 Wilshire, and at Wilshire and Rampart boulevards a splendid Queen Anne-style mansion for Chicago grain merchant Hiram Higgins. The Higgins mansion is the only example of these early Wilshire Boulevard homes to survive, beautifully intact two miles west at 637 S. Lucerne Boulevard in the Windsor Square neighborhood. It was cut into three pieces and relocated on a Friday night in 1923, accompanied by the mayor and friends of the owners who celebrated inside one of the truck-borne sections. The Kress House Moving Co., which did the job, boasted that it was the largest residence ever relocated west of the Mississippi River.

As the boulevard's affluence grew, land speculators began to see an unlimited future to the west. Two years after Wilshire Boulevard's establishment, the town boundary at Hoover Street was pushed another half-mile west to Vermont Avenue. The boulevard followed, extended past Sunset Park to the new city limits and given a corrective forty-five-

The Hancock family's music salon at Villa Madonna came with a renowned pipe organ. The room where orchestras gave recitals has been preserved at the University of Southern California.

degree turn to the left so it would align better with the compass. Another jump west mapped the boulevard's course a-mile-and-a-half out to Irving Boulevard, named for banker Irving Hellman. This new leg was originally labeled Sixth Street, a sign that not everybody yet agreed on Wilshire Boulevard's potential as a major thoroughfare. Many of the city's best-known figures did, though, and built their mansions along the westward extension of Wilshire Boulevard.

Explorer and music patron G. Allan Hancock lived in Villa Madonna after his mother Ida Hancock Ross died in 1913, just before its completion on the northeast corner of Wilshire and Vermont Avenue. He and his wife moved out after their son died in a 1925 Santa Barbara earthquake.

Leading lawyer Henry W. O'Melveny lived at 3250 Wilshire in an English Arts and Crafts-style home with eight bedrooms designed by architect Sumner Hunt. Marco Hellman, the banker who gently dismissed Gaylord Wilshire's 1920s real estate aspirations, occupied the southwest corner of Wilshire and Catalina Avenue. His brother Irving lived across the street. The so-called oil queen of California Emma A. Summers, who controlled half the gushers around downtown Los Angeles, bought a mansion at the intersection with Wilshire Place. When automobiles and new streetcar lines began to make living farther from town more attractive, Wilshire became even more popular. Barney Oldfield, the West's most celebrated auto racer, lived at Wilshire and Ardmore Avenue. Thomas Ince, the early motion picture mogul, called the southwest corner of Wilshire and Hobart boulevards his home.

"Many fine homes of our best citizens now adorn Wilshire Boulevard," the *Times* reported on March 28, 1909.

Despite the boulevard's elevated stature, drivers had to be alert for ruts and sinkholes, especially west of the settled area. "Have we no civic pride? Wilshire Boulevard has never been a good road," the *Los Angeles Examiner* protested. Hazards included wandering sheep, sharp dips and a narrow bridge over Sacatella Creek, a riparian thicket of tules and frogs that crossed the boulevard at Mariposa Avenue. The creek spilled out of Bimini Slough, a wild swale that cleaved the northwestern reaches of the city before stopping just above the boulevard at Sixth Street and Alexandria Avenue. An early real estate development called Chapman Park planted itself along Wilshire between Catalina Avenue and Normandie Street, at the mouth of the slough, on the

Austin's rambling brick Hershey Arms brought a taste of English Renaissance to the original Wilshire Tract. Its 1907 opening began the boulevard's shift away from purely residential use.

Hotel Hershey Arms, Wilshire Boulevard, Los Angeles, Cal.

promise that a new scenic drive up through the ravine would connect the boulevard to the Silver Lake reservoir, three miles away. The Silver Lake Parkway never got finished, but Chapman Park became a prominent neighborhood, built on extensive earth fill that transformed the slough from a flood-prone vehicular obstacle into flat ground level and dry enough for homes and streets. The tract was built by the family that later lent its name to Southern California's Chapman University and that donated land for the Wilshire Christian Church at Normandie Avenue.

Gaylord Wilshire had left town without seeing his boulevard grow, but there were others envisioning great things. That Wilshire Boulevard would eventually reach the Pacific, more than fourteen miles from General Otis's home, was foreseen in a persuasive 1907 blueprint for the future of Los Angeles streets. Charles Mulford Robinson, an advocate of the City Beautiful movement, enthused that "Wilshire . . . is more boulevard-like than anything Los Angeles has." He urged that its entire length to the coast be imagined impressively wide with an ample median parkway of attractive trees and flowers. He also suggested that the intersection at Wilshire and Vermont be exalted with a *rond-point*, or traffic circle, of Parisian inspiration and scale.

"It is clear that the junction point of these two boulevards is of a civic significance which should be marked," Robinson wrote. His ideas for beautifying the city's roads took up three full news pages in the *Times*. Not all were enacted, but his passion instilled the confidence in prominent citizens that Wilshire would be a vital boulevard in the city's future.

He did predict correctly that Vermont and

Interior, Hershey Arms — Wilshire Boulevard, Los Angeles, Cal.

While downtown hotels were serious and traditional, the airy Hershey Arms featured exotic furnishings and semitropical gardens. It became popular with winter visitors and society women.

The new Wilshire District began to fill in around Westlake Park.
The boulevard stopped at the park's western boundary (foreground)
until a viaduct reduced the lake's size in 1934. Sixth Street
adjoins the park on the left, Seventh Street on the right.

Wilshire would turn into a major crossroads. The meeting of the two streets became one of the city's most heavily traveled intersections, its stature elevated by a mansion the *Times* called in 1913 "the most sumptuous home in Los Angeles." John C. Austin, of course, got the commission for Villa Madonna, which sat atop a high driveway on the northeast corner. He designed a twenty-three-room mansion with dual entry steps and rich in exquisite touches. European and Asian art and imported furnishings filled the home. The music salon, featuring a large Wurlitzer pipe organ and Persian rugs, became a celebrated Wilshire Boulevard cultural venue, graced in later years with performances by violin virtuoso Jascha Heifetz and cellists Pablo Casals and Gregor Piatigorsky, among others.

The patron of Villa Madonna, said to be inspired by Villa Medici in Florence, was Ida Haraszthy Hancock Ross, a respected philanthropist and society figure. The daughter of a Hungarian count and a Polish noblewoman, she migrated to Los Angeles as a girl by wagon on the Santa Fe Trail. She later married Major Henry Hancock, a much older state legislator and the region's official land surveyor. After his death in 1883, she and their son G. Allan Hancock ran the family's vast land holdings, including the three-thousand-acre *Rancho La Brea* where they lived in an adobe beside the tar pits west of the city. The *brea* and shallow oil fields produced income, but the Hancocks did not become cash wealthy until they began selling off chunks of the rancho to speculators who developed the communities of Hollywood and Windsor Square, among others. Mrs. Hancock, who had remarried federal judge Erskine M. Ross, did not live to see the mansion's heyday. She died in 1913 just as Villa Madonna was completed.

MANSIONS BUILT BY prominent Los Angeles citizens and retirees from the East, their wealth not yet diluted by a national income tax, pushed the value of Wilshire Boulevard land to lofty heights. Inevitably, the four blocks of the original tract between Westlake and Sunset parks became too desirable to remain the exclusive preserve of private homes. As occurred in other American cities with grand avenues, investors swooped in with generous offers to buy up the residences, relocate or raze them, and build luxury apartments and hotels. This trend began as early as 1907 to change the face of the boulevard and create the beginnings of a recognizable Wilshire skyline.

The first big establishment, the Hershey Arms hotel, rose two blocks west of the Otis residence, on the south side of the boulevard between Coronado and Rampart. It was open and inviting in the way downtown's stolid hotels were not, with exotic furnishings and a semitropical garden. The Hershey Arms filled the entire block and became a center of society life. Guests in the hundred or so mahogany-furnished rooms might stay a week, an entire season or take up occupancy indefinitely.

The hotel's name came from Mira Hershey, an intriguing figure in Los Angeles history who had come west from Muscatine, Iowa, in the 1890s with a sizable inheritance from her father. (They may have been distantly related to the Hershey chocolate family, later prominent in Pennsylvania.) She helped to design several attractive houses on Bunker Hill, the affluent heights above downtown, and would later run the landmark Hollywood Hotel and invest wisely enough in land to be snidely referred to in the papers as "mistress of millions." When she died in 1930, her will left sizable amounts to hospitals and the county science museum, but the biggest gift, four hundred thousand dollars, endowed Mira Hershey Hall, the first women's dormitory at UCLA.

For the Hershey Arms, she commissioned John C. Austin to build an English Renaissance brick edifice with peaked roofs and whimsical angles. Hershey herself never ran the hotel, instead leasing it for several years to another intriguing woman of the time. Helen Mathewson served as president of the city's Humane Animal League and was known, through the newspapers, as something of a civic scold on the treatment of horses and stray pets. Her tastes ran to Japanese furniture and teakwood, which gave the hotel an exotic feel. Mathewson was progressive for the time, employing African Americans when most hotels practiced segregation. Vada Jetmore Somerville, the first black female dentist in Los Angeles and later the proprietor of the famous Dunbar Hotel on Jazz-Age Central Avenue, kept the Hershey Arms books for six years.

The Hershey Arms only lasted until the 1950s, but its early success encouraged the rise of a fashionable hotel and apartment district. *Architect and Engineer* magazine praised this trend in a 1913 report that posed the question, "Why is it that Los Angeles builds better apartment houses than San Francisco?" The accolade concerned a pair of apartment-hotels that still tower above the north side of Wilshire at Rampart Boulevard. The Rampart came first, constructed close to Sixth Street in 1910 by builder Hugh W. Bryson. Two years later he sold the property to concentrate on building his more noteworthy namesake, the Bryson, where a double pair of heraldic lions in front of a white-marble Beaux Arts façade gazes upon Wilshire Boulevard. The Bryson has survived to be listed on the National Register of Historic Places.

Each of the ninety-six original apartments featured mahogany woodwork, hideaway wall beds, tile baths and kitchens, and built-in cedar chests. Furnishings included china and silver service for six, even champagne glasses and finger bowls. On the top floor was a ballroom and glassed-in loggia that, on clear days, offered views of distant Catalina Island. The Bryson was fully occupied two days after the official opening on January 10, 1913, defying skeptics who called Los Angeles too provincial to support such a deluxe building. The *Times* proclaimed the Bryson "by far the largest and finest apartment house on the Pacific Coast" and praised its location on "one of the most sightly corners in the fashionable Wilshire-Westlake district." When Bryson sold the property for nine hundred fifty thousand dollars, it was reported as Los Angeles's richest real estate transaction of 1913.

Raymond Chandler paid homage to the Bryson in one of his noir detective mysteries, *The Lady in the Lake*, taking some fictional license with the details:

> *He drove down to Wilshire and we turned east again. Twenty-five minutes brought us to the Bryson Tower, a white stucco palace with fretted lanterns in the forecourt and tall date palms. The entrance was in an L, up marble steps, through a Moorish archway, and over a lobby that was too big and a carpet that was too blue. Blue Ali Baba oil jars were dotted around, big enough to keep tigers in. There was a desk and a night clerk with one of those mustaches that get stuck under your fingernail.*

Across Rampart Boulevard to the east stands another sturdy survivor. Opened in 1927 as the

Arcady, it later operated as Fifield Manor, the Wilshire Royale and a Howard Johnson hotel. The original Arcady had been built on the site of the relocated Higgins mansion by Olive Philips, a member of the city parks commission and stalwart of the Woman's Christian Temperance Union.

The district's most visually spectacular piece of architecture, then and now, appeared on the skyline beside Westlake Park in 1925. From anywhere in that part of the city, the eleven-story etched-concrete hulk guarded by soaring warrior angels provided a dazzling sight. Lodge 99 of the Benevolent and Protective Order of Elks was built as a private retreat for the power elite.

So many politicians, judges and powerful figures haunted the opulent clubrooms and halls overlooking the park that wags called it City Hall West. The Elks Lodge was built during the Egyptian Revival excitement that followed the breathtaking discovery of King Tut's tomb—and it shows. Designed by architects Alexander Curlett and Claude Beelman, the exterior sports an abundance of visual flourishes—tall plinths that morph into behemoth angels, a frieze of fierce-eyed soldiers circling the building, a dramatic arched entrance. Inside is no less spectacular. The ceiling of the vaulted marble lobby is covered in a mural of classical Greek figures painted by young Anthony Heinsbergen, a Dutch-born artist who would go on to execute acclaimed works on Wilshire Boulevard and around Los Angeles, including in the City Hall. He once told an interviewer, "After the Elks job, I did not have to solicit a single job for thirty-eight years." Since the Elks sold the lodge in the 1960s, it has served as a hotel and locale for weddings and other festive events, as well as a popular movie filming location for Hollywood.

AS HE ATE BREAKFAST in bed at his son Harry Chandler's home on July 30, 1917, Harrison Gray Otis announced to his nurse "I am gone" and passed away. Long widowed and eighty years old, he had lived out his final years mostly at his ranch in the San Fernando Valley. Rather than leave the Bivouac at Wilshire and Park View sitting vacant, he had begun making arrangements to donate the property to the County of Los Angeles for the "interests of art, artists, art-loving people and other devotees of their higher aims and causes which specifically appertain to the finer side of life." In other words, an art school.

County officials were not certain they wanted to operate such a school, and they did not get around to opening the Otis Art Institute until September 27, 1920. In its early years, Otis was an arm of the public art museum in Exposition Park. Students gathered in the former family rooms for classes in painting, sculpture, ceramics, photography and fashion design. A fixture under various names and ownership for seventy-seven years, with a long roster of accomplished alumni, Otis anchored a creative district around Westlake Park that attracted artist studios, other schools such as Art Center (where photographer Ansel Adams taught), architects and galleries. The Earl Stendahl Gallery, five blocks west at 3006 Wilshire Boulevard, became a cutting-edge art showcase. Stendahl's most talked-about exhibition presented Pablo Picasso and his controversial *Guernica*, an antiwar mural depicting images of weeping women and a baby's corpse intended to protest the bombardment of a Basque town by fascists in the Spanish Civil War of the 1930s.

When the artists arrived, Westlake Park already sported a slightly Bohemian air. It had become a grassy enclave in the expanding city, popular with self-styled preachers, sybarites and eccentrics. "A vast amount of therapeutic lore was to be had for nothing in Westlake Park," is how a 1920s novel *The Boosters* described the habitués. "The elderly men and women, hailing chiefly from the Mississippi watershed, who had made this pleasance their daily rendezvous, were walking encyclopedias of medical knowledge. They seem to have experienced all ailments, tried all cures." It was in this milieu that the Otis Institute's chief rival for students and eminence in the Westlake art world also began.

The Chouinard Art Institute was founded by Nelbert Murphy Chouinard, who had briefly taught art history at Otis. She opened her own school in 1921 and attracted future painters such as Edward Ruscha and Lita Albuquerque and film animator Chuck Jones. For one year the faculty included Modernist architects Richard Neutra and Rudolf M. Schindler, both on the rise as important figures. While Otis was thought of as a more sedate institution, Chouinard enjoyed a progressive reputation. Some of that image was due to the inflamed reaction that greeted Mexican muralist David Alfaro Siqueiros, invited by Mrs.

Chouinard to be an artist in residence in 1932. He was welcomed onto the art jury for the Olympic Games held in Los Angeles that year, but his revolutionary politics ignited controversy over murals he painted on Olvera Street downtown and in the sculpture court of the Chouinard campus at 743 S. Grand View Street.

When his visa ran out, Siqueiros was forced to leave the country and both murals were obliterated. Seventy years later, restorers began uncovering the lost artworks. *Workers' Meeting,* the fresco depicting a proletarian gathering painted at Chouinard, had been believed destroyed until some persistent alumni discovered the mural under layers of paint and a room addition inside what became a Korean church school.

Architects who would greatly influence the style of Wilshire Boulevard also contributed to the Westlake creative scene. Both the former Chouinard campus, which is an official Los Angeles Historic–Cultural Monument, and the French Provincial build-

Art schools flourished around Westlake Park after Otis, shown at left in 1937, began holding classes. Chouinard was located at 743 S. Grand View Street, while the site of the future Art Center College of Design was on nearby Seventh Street. Faculty included young photographer Ansel Adams.

ing that housed the Stendahl Gallery were designed by an architecture firm that shaped the boulevard's aesthetic tone through several eras. Morgan, Walls and Morgan had been an old-line Los Angeles partnership, but the addition of Stiles O. Clements in 1923 as chief designer elevated the firm to new prominence. Led by Clements, the firm's work from the 1920s into the '50s produced dozens of noteworthy commercial buildings. Clements designed the El Capitan Theater in Hollywood and, in downtown, the Mayan Theater and the celebrated Art Deco black-and-gold Richfield Oil building, since demolished. On Wilshire, where Clements had a hand in more than a hundred structures, some of his best work includes the aqua-green terra-cotta Pellissier building and Wiltern Theater at Western Avenue, listed on the National Register of Historic Places, and the Dominguez-Wilshire tower on the Miracle Mile.

Though he often goes unappreciated, Clements's oeuvre in several architectural styles—Spanish Revival and playful Churrigueresque, French Provincial, Zigzag Moderne and Streamline Moderne among them—expressed many of the forces that were fashioning the Los Angeles of the future during his career: commercialism, popular culture, the automobile, suburbia. "Stiles O. Clements is one of Los Angeles's most important architects," according to architectural historian Alan Hess. "L.A. architects led the nation in creating a new architecture for the auto beginning in the 1920s [and] Clements stands in the first rank."

In the mid-1950s, the original Otis mansion and the Earl home next door were torn down to make way for an expanded, modern art campus. Instead of an inviting lawn softening the corner of Wilshire and Park View, a three-story wall of travertine hid roomy new classrooms and studios. It was a clear sign of changing times in Gaylord Wilshire's original tract. Things got crowded for the first time. Models that had posed nude on the Otis roof were chased indoors by the prying eyes of office workers in the American Cement Co. headquarters, constructed across Wilshire. The Hershey Arms hotel was torn down for another office building, a boxy rectangle devoid of visual interest.

Whether devoted to more intensive business uses or, later, to a densely populated immigrant community plagued by high crime rates, the Westlake District became less receptive to art students. Chouinard merged with the Los Angeles Conservatory of Music to form the California Institute for the Arts, leaving for the suburbs in 1972. Otis stayed longer, expanding again in 1988 after merging with New York's Parsons School of Design. Three years later the Los Angeles side of the partnership broke off to become the Otis College of Art and Design. Finally, it too departed Wilshire Boulevard in 1997 for a fresh start close to the ocean near Los Angeles International Airport.

All that remains from General Otis's time at his corner of Wilshire and Park View is a single date palm, fully grown in the Wilshire parkway. The former art institute has been remodeled into a public elementary school. Next door, what used to be the Elks Lodge became the Park Plaza hotel, a popular venue for parties and location filming for Hollywood studios. The American Cement building's offices on the southwest corner have been converted to work-live lofts. If General Otis were around, he would be lucky to recognize anything, even the city parks he knew so well.

Sunset Park, at the west end of the Wilshire tract, was renamed following World War I for Marie

STILES O. CLEMENTS

Welton Becket, John C. Austin and the father-and-son team of John and Donald Parkinson all helped shape Wilshire Boulevard's eclectic skyline. No architectural legacy, however, matches the range of commercial work executed by Stiles O. Clements. Born in Maryland in 1883, he became an Angeleno in 1911 and guided Los Angeles design into the modern era.

Clements joined the city's most prolific architecture firm in 1923, after the death of founder Octavius Morgan. As chief designer he steered the renamed Morgan, Walls and Clements into a leading role on Wilshire Boulevard. Spanish Revival was becoming a defining Wilshire look—out of necessity. The emerging boulevard needed eye appeal to lure shoppers away from downtown. Clements embellished on the basics by introducing playful Churrigueresque flourishes.

Mysterious monkeys grin from around the windows of his 1926 studio building at Wilshire and Berendo Street. The 1923 McKinley Building at Oxford Avenue, demolished in 1998, included a loggia and a hidden inner courtyard that delighted shoppers. Clements came up with a distinctive Spanish palace motif for grocer George A. Ralphs, whose 1928 market on Wilshire's new Miracle Mile featured Baroque and Medieval detailing and Gothic arches.

As tastes changed, Clements decorated Wilshire and other boulevards with memorable Art Deco, French Provincial and Late Moderne stores and office buildings. His elegant Mullen and Bluett department store at Wilshire and Harvard drew raves in 1930, and later in the decade *California Arts and Architecture* magazine lauded Morgan, Walls and Clements for having "done so much . . . to beautify the business streets of Los Angeles."

Clements remained active on Wilshire projects until leaving the firm in his son's hands in 1965. He died the following year. Only recently has his contribution to the aesthetic sense of the Automobile Age boulevard begun to be appreciated.

Clements's artistry is apparent in this 1926 Churrigueresque design that still stands at Wilshire and Carondelet Street. Numerous restaurants and the Vagabond theater have been tenants through the years.

Joseph Paul Yves Roch Gilbert du Motier, the French Marquis de Lafayette, who had fought for the colonies in the American Revolution. His statue stands in Lafayette Park as a symbol of French–American friendship. The park's Felipe De Neve branch library, named for the Spanish governor who founded Los Angeles, is listed on the National Register of Historic Places, as is the Spanish Colonial Revival Granada Shoppes and Studios just off Wilshire Boulevard at 672 S. Lafayette Park Place. Built as live-in work spaces in 1927 by Franklin Harper, a journalist turned real estate developer, the complex of four buildings "reeks of panache among Southern California's architecture and design community," says architect and critic Charles W. Moore.

Westlake Park also got a change of identity.

In 1942 it was renamed for Army General Douglas MacArthur, when the aging publisher of the *Los Angeles Examiner* William Randolph Hearst decided the soldier leading America's World War II effort in the Pacific would make a good president. Hearst tapped his chief political writer to orchestrate the change, and by the time the Westlake neighborhood heard of it and began to object, the mayor had already telegraphed MacArthur with the good news and scheduled a parade on Wilshire Boulevard. Once a pleasant escape, MacArthur Park sits at the center of one of the poorest immigrant neighborhoods in the country. The Red Line subway that follows Wilshire Boulevard rattles thirty feet below the lake, now much smaller than in Otis's day. Wilshire Boulevard itself cuts a curving swath across the former walking

ELKS TEMPLE "99", SIXTH AND PARKVIEW STS., LOS ANGELES, CALIFORNIA

160 DE LUXE HOTEL ROOMS OPEN TO THE PUBLIC

The former Elks lodge, later called the Park Plaza hotel, is one of the city's most popular interior filming locations. Hollywood studios appreciate its 1920s styling and oversized stairway and ballrooms.

paths, splitting the old park in two sections—the result of a 1920s master strategy to help traffic move more efficiently through Los Angeles.

One final, evocative reminder of the General Otis era remains at Wilshire and Park View. Posed in flowerbeds at the park entrance on the southeast corner, two bronze figures survey the passing scene, just as they did in the 1921 silent-film short *Hard Luck,* when Buster Keaton eluded the cops by hiding among these same statues. They were struck a year earlier by sculptor Paul Troubetzkoy, whose smaller bronze depicts a newsboy hawking papers. Next to him stands Harrison Gray Otis in full Spanish-American War uniform, sword by his left side, right index finger extended across the intersection at the corner he called home.

Giant warrior angels atop the Elks building dominate the skyline over MacArthur Park, the name given to Westlake Park during World War II at the insistence of newspaper publisher William Randolph Hearst.

The flag-bearing Spanish-American War soldier has disappeared, but statues of Harrison Gray Otis pointing at his former home and a newsboy still stand beside the boulevard at Park View Street.

CHAPTER THREE

GLAMOROUS BOULEVARD

IT TOOK TIME for Wilshire Boulevard to bloom into a fully formed Automobile Age phenomenon. The year that Harrison Gray Otis passed away, a ride out to the sea at Santa Monica still required bumping along a kidney-jarring dirt road. That all changed after the Roaring Twenties blew into town. A more adventurous and expansive spirit swept across Los Angeles, some of it brought by the hundred thousand new arrivals who alighted each year looking for a better life under the palm trees. They bought into what historian Jules Tygiel called the "speculative soul" of the fast-growing city, extracting Los Angeles further from its pueblo roots.

Dazzling new showpieces proclaimed the

Fashion shows and swimming competitions hosted by aquatic celebrities like Johnny Weissmuller and Buster Crabbe attracted star power to the Ambassador Hotel pool. A members' health club and sand beach for sunning were added in 1932.

modern decade. Most spectacular of all was the soaring granite City Hall—454 feet tall, twice as high as anything else on the horizon, topped with a shining beacon. Its gleaming tower became a civic symbol of uninhibited aspiration, a trait also expressed with elan in the Elks Lodge at Westlake Park. Theater impresario Sid Grauman's Chinese and Egyptian theaters brought a playful style to sleepy Hollywood Boulevard. Smoky jazz clubs and roadhouses opened all over town, despite national Prohibition. In this exciting time, Wilshire Boulevard came into its own as a glamorous and trend-setting thoroughfare—wilder than Broadway downtown, tonier than Hollywood or the lawless Sunset Strip.

Some of the credit for Wilshire's garrulous personality belongs to Earle C. Anthony, an underrated player in the Los Angeles story. As a seventeen-year-old, he attached an electric motor to a buckboard and puttered through downtown at six miles an hour, scaring the horses. His was the first

"horseless carriage" that most Angelenos of 1897 had seen. He became a leading automobile dealer, organized the first car show in Southern California and started a chain of gasoline stations. Anthony also made an aesthetic splash in 1909 when he commissioned the prominent Pasadena architects Charles and Henry Greene, innovators of the Craftsman bungalow style, to design a stunning home at Wilshire and Berendo Avenue, six blocks west of what was then still Sunset Park. If it were still on Wilshire, the Greene and Greene home might be lauded as the boulevard's most magnificent architectural landmark. It was sold in 1923, however, and moved to North Bedford Drive in Beverly Hills.

Anthony's more enduring gift to Wilshire's scenery is the electric device he brought back from France to advertise his Packard dealership. The country's first neon sign, blazing in cool blue and orange over a downtown street, caused a sensation. Neon implied modern, so it fit perfectly with the emerging Wilshire sensibility of freedom and loosened inhibition. Before long, signs glowing from rooftops and storefronts defined the visual style of after-dark Los Angeles. "They shriek in your eyes; you long to hush them, to be rid of their blinding clamor, their deafening glare," a *Harper's Monthly* writer protested in the Twenties. She was overruled by Raymond Chandler's grizzled detective Philip Marlowe, no effete art lover, who muttered approvingly in *The Little Sister,* "There ought to be a monument to the man who invented neon lights. There's

Earle C. Anthony attended Los Angeles High School when his half-horsepower electric car made its run. He later became the exclusive California dealer for luxury Packards, but neon signs are his enduring Wilshire legacy.

a boy who really made something out of nothing."

Even before the first neon appeared, Wilshire Boulevard's future as a place of fun and glamour was declared by the opening of the Ambassador Hotel on New Year's Day in 1921. Built in a dairy pasture west of Vermont Avenue, the grounds rambled over twenty-three rising acres. Advertisements pitched the Ambassador as the first country resort to be located inside the city limits of Los Angeles. No one who stayed there ever risked boredom. The Ambassador offered a pitch-and-putt golf course, bowling alley, stables, horse show arena, movie theater and stylish shops such as I. Magnin. For a time the hotel maintained a menagerie of bears, camels and other exotic creatures. The large swimming pool later featured a sandy beach. Guests who required still more entertainment could ask to be driven a few miles west to the hotel's private Rancho Golf Club on Pico Boulevard or to rival airfields at the intersection of Wilshire and Fairfax Avenue.

Originally to be called The California, the hotel had been eagerly awaited. "Completion of this hotel and its magnificent grounds to be in the heart of the fashionable Wilshire district . . . [will] make Los Angeles the 'Paris of America,'" the *Los Angeles Examiner* enthused before the first shovel was lifted. When money ran out during construction, prominent lawyer Henry O'Melveny stepped in to take charge. He arranged new ownership and guided the project ahead. Two days before the doors opened, carpets had not yet been installed. The first guest, a Briton who had sailed from London, nearly got turned away. Almost immediately, however, Los Angeles fell in love with its new jewel. After a gala christening ball, the *Examiner* observed: "Never has a society event in the [city] seen so many dinner parties gathered under one

After the 1921 opening, society families such as the DuPonts and Vanderbilts began to summer at the Ambassador. They were met with fresh flowers at the train stations downtown. Staff with experience at keeping demanding guests happy had to be hired in the East.

Outdoor Life on the South Grounds of the Ambassador, Los Angeles

Architect Myron Hunt dressed up the Ambassador grounds with fifty-year-old
palms and other exotic trees to give the former Schmidt dairy farm
"the appearance of having been in existence for a long time."
Guests could pick fresh bananas, oranges and lemons between games of golf or
chat with movie stars. Actress Pola Negri walked her pet cheetah on the lawns.

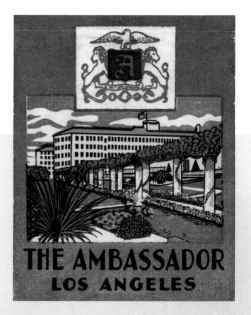

THE AMBASSADOR
LOS ANGELES

Wilshire Boulevard Entrance to Los Angeles Ambassador

As the boulevard filled in, the Ambassador was remodeled to welcome guests arriving by car and limousine. Celebrities, socialites and debutantes all crossed paths in the elegant lobby. Long-term residents included newspaper gossip columnist Walter Winchell and FBI director J. Edgar Hoover.

roof." In his private journal, O'Melveny allowed himself a terse pat on the back: "Probably two thousand people present—wonderfully well managed—good dinner—the dancing presented an interesting sight."

The Ambassador provided the two spheres of moneyed Los Angeles, the proper society families listed in the *Blue Book* and the movie stars whose names blazed on marquees, a common meeting ground. The *New York Telegraph* described a 1921 banquet for the newly formed Screen Writers Guild as the "greatest single social gathering of literary and professional celebrities ever staged." The Ambassador became the venue of choice for Hollywood events such as the Academy Awards, presented there six times, and for grand civic celebrations. Los Angeles feted Charles Lindbergh after his triumphant solo flight across the Atlantic in 1927 with a packed Ambassador ball hosted by William Randolph Hearst and comedic actress Marion Davies, who were not-so-

secretly in the midst of an extramarital affair that lasted thirty years. When the world's largest airship, the *Graf Zeppelin,* stopped in Los Angeles in 1929, the banquet for the passengers and crew drew everyone from the governor and mayor to Hollywood's It couple, Mary Pickford and Douglas Fairbanks.

Architect Myron Hunt had just finished the Huntington Hotel in Pasadena when he was asked to design the Wilshire Boulevard resort. Hunt had abandoned a promising Chicago practice to relocate on the West Coast for his wife's health. As the rare Los Angeles architect with university credentials, he commanded some of the city's highest fees. He designed the graceful Henry Huntington mansion and library in San Marino, the Rose Bowl and Occidental College. For the Ambassador, he proposed an H-shaped main building with Mediterranean-style hipped roofs and tawny plaster exteriors. Every sleeping room and bathroom got a window, some with

Stars could always get a seat—or a spot on stage—at the Cocoanut Grove. Bing Crosby and Jack Benny proposed to their wives among the faux monkeys, Judy Garland recorded an album there and Barbra Streisand made her Los Angeles debut in 1963.

THE COCOANUT GROVE
AMBASSADOR HOTEL, LOS ANGELES.

views of Catalina Island forty miles away.

The Ambassador's notoriety, however, was always rooted more in its lore than its architecture. General Douglas MacArthur remarked there in his farewell speech, "Old soldiers never die, they just fade away." Nikita Khrushchev, premier of the Soviet Union during a heated period of the Cold War, fumed at the Ambassador when he was forbidden to visit Disneyland in 1959. Three years later, a defeated candidate for governor temporarily retired from public life, vowing bitterly in a hotel news conference that the press "would not have Richard Nixon to kick around anymore." When Nixon moved into the White House in 1969, he became the sixth president to have slept at the Ambassador.

Publicists fed free meals and juicy tidbits to reporters to keep the Ambassador in the news. One running story concerned a canary that flew in the window of a longtime resident, Mrs. John E. Bishop. She named the bird Mickey Bishop, enrolled him in the Audubon Society and the Red Cross, and paid for

Harry Belafonte and Lena Horne broke barriers by headlining at the Grove after World War II. But in 1940 when Hattie McDaniel became the first African American to win an Oscar, for *Gone With the Wind*, she sat at a separate table. Check the bottom center of the photograph.

the installation of birdbaths in his honor in nine city parks including Westlake and Lafayette. Most of the lore involves the hijinks of celebrities who socialized in the exclusive bungalows that ringed the grounds, connected by service tunnels to the main building. Writer F. Scott Fitzgerald and his wife Zelda, according to legend, ran out on a bill by piling furniture and

Diners at the original Brown Derby at 3427 Wilshire and facing the Ambassador didn't mind the glorified chili-parlor fare and cramped booths. They did groan at acoustics that let eavesdroppers pry on private conversations.

papers in their room and lighting the pyre. While Albert Einstein was in residence, he investigated a hallway ruckus and found heavyweight boxing champion Jack Dempsey grappling with a woman. Dempsey reportedly stopped and introduced himself, pleased to make the great man's acquaintance. Actress Tallulah Bankhead supposedly accepted a telegram in the nude, then apologized to the delivery boy: "I don't have a tip on me." When Davies rode a white horse through the lobby to amuse Hearst, he was asked later if he had been surprised. "Yes," he

quipped. "She hates horses." The most famous adulterous couple in America rented the entire second floor of the east wing for a year.

Stars came to the Ambassador in part for its legendary dance and supper club, the Cocoanut Grove. Decorated in a faux-Moroccan theme with dangling monkey dolls and fake palm trees, the Grove was packed from the first night. Part of the fun was never knowing when a new star might be discovered or some celebrity drama—a fistfight, a lovers' spat—might flare up. Regulars on Tuesday "star nights" included Pickford, Gloria Swanson, Charlie Chaplin, Howard Hughes, John Barrymore, W.C. Fields and the Talmadge sisters, Norma and Constance, of silent film fame. Joan Crawford's career took off after she won Charleston contests at the Grove under her real name, Lucille Le Sueur. Bing Crosby was said to have been discovered singing at the Grove with a band called the Rhythm Boys.

Young Frank Sinatra appeared first with the Tommy Dorsey Orchestra and later returned as a headliner. "The Cocoanut Grove was a party every night," journalist Adela Rogers St. Johns remarked in *Are the Stars Out Tonight?*, a book by the hotel's retired publicist Margaret Tante Burk.

Customers packing into the Ambassador and the Grove made Wilshire Boulevard a nightlife destination and a recognized, coveted American place. Gossip columns and movie magazines spread the boulevard's fame. The hotel's popularity also led to creation of another long-lasting cultural landmark. Over dinner at the Ambassador one night in 1925, Grauman and two friends, Herbert K. Somborn and Wilson Mizner, commiserated about the dearth of good local restaurants. Movie producer Somborn, recently divorced from Gloria Swanson, had a peevish insistence on food quality. He would bring his own fresh eggs to a restaurant, mark the shells with

THE ORIGINAL BROWN DERBY CAFE   LOS ANGELES, CAL.   -40-

Larger quarters in 1936 came with a newly built hat and patio dining. This Brown Derby at 3377 Wilshire often was mistaken for the original. When the end came abruptly in 1980, preservationists could not save the unofficial boulevard landmark.

his initials, then demand that the kitchen boil them for precisely three minutes. Mizner, a New York wit and raconteur, was less demanding. He mostly longed for a Manhattan-style hangout where his actor and writer pals could tell stories and hurl insults late into the night. With backing from Jack Warner of the Warner Bros. studio, Somborn and Mizner opened the Brown Derby Café at 3427 Wilshire Boulevard, an easy one-block walk for revelers and musicians pouring out of the Cocoanut Grove at closing time.

Conflicting stories are told about the origin of the Brown Derby name. The authorized *Brown Derby Cookbook,* published in 1949, endorsed the version where Somborn assured his partners: "You could open a restaurant in an alley and call it anything, or you could even build in the shape of a hat, and if the food

and service were good the patrons would come flocking." That original Brown Derby didn't become a hit based on creature comforts. Diners squeezed under a thirty-foot-diameter hat made of wood and plaster. The menu offered burgers, hot dogs, melted-cheese sandwiches, chili, tamales, coffee, tea, milk and near beer. Chiffon cake was added when the patrons demanded something sweet; later, a grapefruit cake requested by dieting gossip columnist Louella Parsons became the signature Brown Derby dessert.

Nothing more creative came out of the kitchen until one night when the manager Bob Cobb scavenged for something to snack on. He threw together a chopped salad of found ingredients: head lettuce, romaine, avocado, watercress, tomatoes, cold chicken breast, hard-boiled egg, bacon, chives, cheese and French dressing. He shared the concoction with regulars Grauman, Mizner and newspaperman Gene Fowler, all of whom began to ask for Cobb's secret salad. The name stuck and, with minor alterations,

Wilshire's fourth Brown Derby lasted only a year. Perino's moved in and served haute cuisine (plus pumpernickel cheese bread) from 1932 to 1949, then relocated to a more refined dining room at 4101 Wilshire. Neither Stiles O. Clements-designed building remains.

went on the menu in 1929. Cobb salads have been a mainstay of American restaurants almost ever since.

The Brown Derby formula proved so popular that on Valentine's Day 1929, a second location opened on Vine Street in Hollywood. Gone was the gimmicky hat, replaced by a more upscale menu and a white-tablecloth demeanor. This became the Brown Derby of the stars. Two years later, another Derby opened in Beverly Hills, at the corner of Wilshire Boulevard and Rodeo Drive. In 1936 the original café moved one block east to the northeast corner of Wilshire and Alexandria Avenue, even closer to the Ambassador. The new location sported a reconstructed hat and a conventional dining room. This Brown Derby remained a boulevard institution until the afternoon of September 9, 1980. Just before 4:00 P.M., a lone diner enjoying a trout dish got the news that his meal was on the house but that he had to depart immediately. By five o'clock the longtime staff had been paid their last checks by owner Gloria Daly, Somborn's daughter, and were gone. Despite the efforts of preservationists, the Brown Derby was razed; the only piece saved was the familiar hat, placed atop a Korean restaurant in a mini-mall erected on the same corner.

As THE 1920S ENDED, with Wilshire Boulevard established as a playground, Herbert Somborn became bored with the Brown Derby's celebrity-and-chili formula. He sought to introduce gourmet dining to the boulevard. He opened the upscale Hi-Hat in 1930 in a newly constructed Morgan, Walls and Clements row of stores at Wilshire and Gramercy Drive, ten blocks west of the original Brown Derby. French and pretentious, the Hi-Hat for a brief time rated mention in the gossip columns whenever a Hollywood pal of Somborn's stopped in. But due perhaps to the looming Depression—or maybe he was just bad at French cuisine—the restaurant never caught on.

Somborn gave up on the Hi-Hat after just a year. In its place, a fourth Wilshire Boulevard location of the Brown Derby was tried, but that proved to be one more than the market could bear. It too soon closed. Somborn, though, was onto something. His misfortune turned into the boulevard's good luck.

The restaurant space came into the hands of a former *maitre d'* at New York's Plaza Hotel. Alex Perino had also served as headwaiter at the prestigious Victor Hugo in downtown Los Angeles. He proved to be the innovator who would turn Wilshire Boulevard into a must-see stop for traveling gourmands. Perino served refined dishes and demanded the freshest ingredients, catering to a cultured clientele in beautiful, if fussy, surroundings—with prices that drew gasps from the unprepared. "It's no place to dine if you're on a budget, but one of the finest if you are celebrating something," *Westways* magazine pronounced in 1939, when a typical daily menu might include soup *a la petite marmite,* broiled baby squab, filet of sole Marguery and iced fruit *au kirsch.*

The original location closed in 1949 and is frequently left out of Perino's lore. The exterior can be glimpsed through a tailor shop window, however, in the film *Sunset Blvd.* when William Holden's character shops for a suit. Perino's moved four blocks west to Wilshire and Norton Avenue, on the edge of the Windsor Square neighborhood. Architects Morgan, Walls and Clements had designed this space as well, some years earlier, as a Thriftimart grocery store. For the new Perino's, the former store got a complete makeover by architect Paul R. Williams. He fashioned a graceful upswept mansard façade, a porte cochere supported by wrought iron flamingos and one of the city's most exquisite dining rooms. Carpeted and serene, it was a soothing oval shape decorated in subtle peach tones, with tailored booths and crystal chandeliers. *Holiday* magazine pronounced this second-generation Perino's, rebuilt after a 1955 fire, "one of the first places for which a traveling gourmet heads when he arrives in Los Angeles." Perino sold in 1969, but the establishment continued for two more decades under new ownership. Even after it closed, the dining room remained a favorite shooting location for film and television studios seeking to recreate the elegance of mid-century Los Angeles. Wreckers razed Perino's in 2005 to make way for apartments.

Anchored by Perino's and the Brown Derby,

Wilshire Boulevard grew a restaurant district comparable to the best in the city. Ollie Hammond's, Cassell's, the Mona Lisa and Lindy's became household names. Lindy's, located at 3656 Wilshire Boulevard, got an unexpected publicity boost in 1940 through a scandal involving notorious gangster Bugsy Siegel. The *Los Angeles Examiner* discovered that while Siegel was supposed to be in the county jail awaiting trial for murder, he was quietly being escorted out of lockup for various appointments around town. A photographer followed one day and snapped photos of prisoner Siegel, dressed in an expensive suit and silk tie, lunching at Lindy's with an attractive actress. When the pictures ran on the front page, heads rolled at the jail—and Lindy's became more crowded.

With the Ambassador's success, Wilshire also

ZEBRA ROOM

Stripes adorned everything at the Zebra Room, the supper club advertised as the place to "meet the world's smartest Smart Set." It was on the ground floor of the dignified Town House at Lafayette Park.

ZEBRA ROOM — THE TOWN HOUSE — LOS ANGELES, CALIFORNIA

grew into a high-status hotel and apartment row. The rambling Spanish-style Chapman Park Hotel, which served as the Olympic village for female athletes competing in the 1932 Games, expanded onto the site of the original Brown Derby, filling an entire block. It was a prominent boulevard landmark until being razed for a high-rise office tower in the 1960s. One block east, the thirteen-story Gaylord Hotel and Apartments had gone up concurrently with the Ambassador—in early photographs they form a lonely skyline surrounded by vacant fields. "Directly across from the Cocoanut Grove," ads for the Gaylord exclaimed. Nearby at Wilshire and Berendo, where Earl C. Anthony's Greene and Greene home had stood, the elegant Talmadge apartments were designed by the architects of the Elks Lodge at Westlake Park. The

Talmadge rented in its heyday to society matrons, business leaders and entertainment figures. The brick tower got its name from Norma Talmadge, the silent film actress who resided there for a time with her husband, studio executive Joseph M. Schenck.

At Wilshire and Bronson Avenue, just west of the final Perino's, another attractive survivor of the 1920s can claim a prestigious entry in the National Register of Historic Places. The Los Altos Apartments were another haunt of William Randolph Hearst and Marion Davies, who had lavish quarters designed there by Julia Morgan, the first female architect in California. "A new standard of beauty and dignity in

When architect Edward B. Rust designed the Los Altos, shown during paving work on Bronson Avenue in 1926, Wilshire Boulevard did not yet have street lights. The apartments have been restored to their original glamour and the building is listed on the National Register of Historic Places.

Los Angeles apartment-house construction," the *Times* said in 1926 of the five-story Spanish Revival building with Italian influences.

Built three years later facing Lafayette Park, the Beaux Arts-style Town House is also listed in the National Register. Opened by prominent Los Angeles oil man Edward Doheny, the Town House began life as an apartment-hotel. Doheny advertised it as "Southern California's most distinguished address," with meals served in the dignified Wedgewood Room, and the Town House did exude a certain regal style. In 1937 the Town House relaunched as a luxury hotel, with a first-floor nightclub, the jam-packed Zebra Room, designed by architect Wayne McAllister and decorated in endless white-and-black stripes. Hotelier Conrad Hilton took over in 1942, and it was there that his son Nicky and young film star Elizabeth Taylor celebrated their marriage. Before his death in 1976, eccentric billionaire Howard Hughes rented out two floors as his private enclave during his period as a germ-fearing recluse.

In time the Town House sold again and was operated as the Sheraton Town House and later as the Sheraton West. It finally closed in 1993, a victim of declining interest in the Roaring Twenties hotels of Wilshire Boulevard. Ultimately, not even the Ambassador—the *grande dame* of Wilshire Boulevard—could outlast the changing times. Never an easy business play, the hotel fell into receivership during the Depression and lingered in financial limbo until its sale in 1946 to J. Myer Schine, a movie theater operator who outbid Conrad Hilton. His son, G. David Schine, managed the hotel after being embroiled in the McCarthy-era political scandals that rocked Washington in the 1950s. Schine also dabbled in Hollywood as an occasional actor and,

later, as the executive producer of the Oscar-winning *The French Connection*. The Schine family tried several times to sell the Ambassador or develop the land, without success.

The hotel's eventual demise can be traced to the assassination of Senator Robert F. Kennedy of New York on June 5, 1968. Just after midnight, Kennedy thanked supporters in the Embassy Ballroom for helping him win the previous day's presidential primary. With California's delegates, the forty-two-year-old Kennedy seemed sure to be the Democrats' candidate against Nixon. After he finished speaking, the plan was for Kennedy to shake some hands then slip into a room to take questions from reporters. Instead, an aide innocently steered Kennedy through the backstage kitchen. When he stopped in a crowded pantry area, a young man stepped from behind an ice machine and fired a .22-caliber revolver. Kennedy fell in a pool of blood, struck once in the head and twice in the torso. Five others in the pantry were wounded before mortified onlookers—among them the National Football League's Roosevelt Grier and the 1960 Olympic decathlon champion, Rafer Johnson—disarmed the gunman. He was Sirhan Bishara Sirhan, a twenty-four-year-old Jordanian immigrant with Palestinian sympathies.

As Kennedy lay wounded, a teenage busboy named Juan Romero placed his rosary beads around the senator's left thumb. When Kennedy's wife, Ethel, pregnant with their eleventh child, reached her husband, he looked up and asked weakly, "Am I all right?" An ambulance sped Kennedy down Wilshire to Good Samaritan Hospital, where he died the following day as supporters prayed in the street outside. Things were never the same at the Ambassador. People stayed away, but in truth the hotel had been faltering for years. The end of World War II had doomed the

Cocoanut Grove. Los Angeles gave up big band dancing for television, rock 'n' roll and tucking the kids into bed in the suburbs. Performer Sammy Davis Jr. tried in 1970 to revive the scene by reinventing the room as the Now Grove with a glitzy Las Vegas sheen, but the new concept never caught on.

Rooms in the main building were closed to guests in May 1987. Bungalows and cottages remained open, but got only light use. Even this unkind existence ceased on January 3, 1989, ending a run of sixty-eight years and two days. That final afternoon, streams of former guests—honeymooners, debutantes, prom queens—walked the halls for a last look around. Tucked under the door of Taffy's, a shop on the casino level, was a thirty-dollar check and a note apologizing for the theft of a blouse sixteen years earlier. For more than a decade, the fate of the Ambassador Hotel was debated. In the end, Robert Kennedy's family asked that the buildings be mostly razed and the grounds be converted into a much needed school for children in the neighborhood.

SEVEN BLOCKS EAST of the Ambassador, another Wilshire Boulevard cultural landmark rose at the end of the 1920s. Quite a few Los Angeles architecture aficionados, and many ex-customers, consider the Bullock's Wilshire department store to be the most exemplary specimen of Art Deco-era splendor ever built in the city. It was the first department store in the country to be designed with the automobile-driving customer in mind—perfect for the emerging Wilshire Boulevard. It served a shared purpose as well, to be a jewel on the Wilshire skyline that lured the city west.

There was no escaping the store's significance once the doors opened at 9:00 A.M. on September 26, 1929. Invited guests applauded and raised champagne flutes to the architects, artisans and visionaries who had presented Los Angeles with a breathtaking expression of the city's emerging aesthetic identity. Bullock's Wilshire joined City Hall as an icon to be flaunted in magazine photo spreads. Bathed in accolades, Bullock's Wilshire showed the country that Los Angeles should be considered a worthy center of design. That opening week, more than a hundred thousand visitors drove to Wilshire Boulevard and Westmoreland Avenue, just west of Lafayette Park, to see what all the fuss was about.

You couldn't miss it. Bullock's Wilshire tantalized the eyes unlike anything else in town, a five-story edifice of buff-hued terra cotta with vertical recesses and copper spandrels, out of which reached a luminous verdigris-coated spire that pierced the sky. At night floodlights washed up the hollow 241-foot tower, and mercury-vapor beacons threw out a violet-blue invitation to the entire city: come see what's happening on Wilshire Boulevard!

Reviewers enthused that the inspiring lines spoke to the forward-looking, optimistic spirit of America—bold, inquiring, aspiring. Inside the store was even more thrilling. "Every detail, from drinking fountain to clock, ventilator grille, mirror hinge, has been creatively evoked from the future and not from the past," Pauline G. Schindler wrote in *California Arts and Architecture. Los Angeles Saturday Night*, the chronicle of 1920s society, pronounced the store a "cathedral of commerce . . . a concrete expression of faith in the boulevard's rich destiny."

Original plans envisioned a much plainer statement. Those plans were redrawn, however, after architect Donald Parkinson and Bullock's executive P.G. Winnett traveled to Paris and became excited

about the graceful yet startling Art Deco designs that debuted at the 1925 *L'Exposition Internationale des Arts Decoratifs et Industriels Modernes.* The exhibition's celebration of the modern inspired a generation of architects, artists and designers to try bold new creations. Young Parkinson and his partner–father John Parkinson set out to elevate the first Wilshire department store to exalted status, to build an Art Deco palace. They possessed the requisite clout to propose and execute such a memorable project. The Parkinsons had provided the concept for City Hall and had designed the Los Angeles Memorial Coliseum and the University of Southern California campus. Fortunately, the chief executive of Bullock's believed that investing in artistic excellence did not hurt business, but rather enhanced the selling of merchandise.

John G. Bullock was a story in himself. He had come to Los Angeles from Ontario, Canada, in 1896, at the age of twenty-five, and talked his way into a job at The Broadway downtown. The Broadway stood out among Los Angeles merchants because proprietor Arthur Letts set fixed prices, which freed customers from the pressure of haggling. At a time when stores customarily rounded off prices to the nickel, Letts charged to the penny. Some of the Broadway's success was due to customers coming in to receive shiny copper pennies in change. Letts's hiring of young J.G. Bullock launched a remarkable business relationship that would reshape the city.

Letts was approached in 1906 by publisher Edwin Tobias Earl—the Wilshire neighbor of Harrison

Many in 1929 hailed Bullock's Wilshire as the city's most beautiful building, while others saw only a fool's gamble. A department store in a residential district would draw little walk-in traffic. But the tallest tower outside of downtown made it easy for drivers to find. Blocks of new stores soon replaced the homes.

Bullock's Wilshire had the first department store windows aimed at drivers instead of sidewalk shoppers. Ads promoted the "era of the future in store design . . . a tribute to far-thinking vision, unremitting devotion and infinite attention to detail."

Gray Otis—who needed a tenant for a building he owned at Seventh Street and Broadway. Earl suggested that Letts expand his store there. Rather than move The Broadway, Letts summoned Bullock and assigned him to establish an entirely new store that would appeal to a more affluent clientele. Letts provided the two-hundred-fifty-thousand-dollar stake and exerted no control—not even over the name. The first Bullock's opened on March 4, 1907, decorated with fresh violets, which signaled the emphasis, entirely unheard of in Los Angeles, on fine goods and cordial personal service. For years after, Bullock's customers received violets on the store's anniversary.

Before long, a thousand of the city's most discriminating shoppers held Bullock's charge accounts. By 1919, Bullock's ranked as the largest

The Wilshire store bore no relation to the downtown Bullock's. The boulevard style was refined and doting. Original artwork gave each floor its own personality.

retail store in the West. There was, however, a flaw in the business plan. The store was rooted downtown while Los Angeles was on its way to becoming a "decentralized city unlike any other in America," in the words of urban planning expert William Fulton. Someday soon, shoppers would choose to shop closer to their homes, which were located ever farther from

Travertine floors and St. Genevieve marble in the dramatic first-floor Perfume Hall alerted patrons that Bullock's Wilshire valued beauty and design above mere commerce. Yet it was a true department store with fur salons, toys, a mezzanine Doggery for canine accessories and the city's first leisurewear merchandise on the Playdeck.

The store itself rises only five stories, but the unoccupied tower soars another ten. Architects John and Donald Parkinson got around the legal height limit by claiming ninety-one feet for signage, a penthouse and roof. They also designed for future expansion.

downtown. Bullock's and rival May Company had bought lots at Wilshire and Vermont in the mid-1920s and talked of erecting massive stores, but abandoned their plans. The first department store to venture outside of downtown, B.H. Dyas and Co., opened in 1928 on Hollywood Boulevard, a developing center of popular shops that lacked the cheap land necessary to dedicate acres to automobile parking.

Wilshire Boulevard, however, had plenty of open land. In a bold stroke that startled financiers, Bullock took his company public, selling $8.5 million in stocks and bonds in two hours. He raised enough cash to buy up a block occupied by the home of oil queen Emma A. Summers. His store was not a branch of the downtown Bullock's, but an entirely new retail concept. It was located in a mostly residential district and catered to the automobile culture. Traditional display windows faced the sidewalk, but they were decorated to catch the eye of motorists. Since most customers would arrive by vehicle, the most appealing entrance was placed in the rear. Under the city's first department store porte cochere, valets in livery welcomed patrons and parked their cars.

Shoppers entered a foyer with travertine floors and elevators finished in nickel, brass and gunmetal. Ahead was the vaulted Perfume Hall, awash in natural light muted by walls of St. Genevieve marble. The decorators, among them the esteemed team of Joseph Feil and Bernard Paradise, Jock Peters and Eleanor Le Maire, had delicately matched color, light and proportion. Clothes and accessories were displayed in low glass cases on rosewood stands or on live mannequins—no hanging racks cluttered the sight lines. Subtle details ruled throughout. The women's shoe salon was paneled with the wood from a single Central American tree. Cork in exotic shades lined the

wall in the furs atelier. The Saddle Shop featured vermilion floor tiles, wall cases of deep red oak and a life-sized plaster likeness of a horse, Bullock's Barney.

Upstairs showrooms and salons functioned almost as discrete boutiques. The Louis XVI Room sold designer dresses, the Directoire formal wear and later furs. Later still came the couture Chanel Room and the Irene Salon, enclave of Hollywood costume designer Irene Gibbons, reputed to be the first boutique devoted to a single designer inside a major U.S. department store. All over the store, service was deferential. Sales associates dressed impeccably, wore

Above the Bullock's Wilshire sidewalk entrance a relief includes the creed: "To build a business that will never know completion." Designer George Stanley was an Otis Art Institute teacher who sculpted the original statuette for the Academy Awards.

gloves as they entered and left, and acted like ladies. As young women, First Lady Patricia Nixon and actress Angela Lansbury served stints on the floor. Hollywood stars loved the doting service. Silent screen heroine Zasu Pitts made flamboyant arrivals at the porte cochere in her vintage Stanley Steamer. Greta Garbo shocked sales associates by visiting in nothing but a trench coat to try on bathing suits.

For refreshment there was the top-floor, desert-themed tearoom and the adjoining lounge where society women gathered for luncheon fashion shows. Truly elite service was reserved for the selected men invited to shop in the privacy of J.G. Bullock's wood-paneled private suite on the fifth floor. Titans of business and politics relaxed over cocktails and hors d'oeuvres as sales associates modeled potential gifts.

The success of Bullock's Wilshire nudged other traditional downtown clothing purveyors to make the move west. In 1930 Mullen and Bluett hired Morgan, Walls and Clements to design a two-story French Provincial store at the corner of Wilshire and Harvard boulevards. Farther west, Desmond's and Silverwoods opened big stores on the Miracle Mile. Small shops catering to discriminating shoppers opened near Bullock's. Cannell and Chaffin, the city's premier decorators, occupied the same building as the Stendahl Gallery. By 1939, Wilshire Boulevard was the finest shopping district in Southern California.

That year, a formidable competitor to Bullock's Wilshire opened three blocks west at New Hampshire Avenue in an all-marble palace designed by Myron Hunt, architect of the Ambassador Hotel. The San Francisco-based I. Magnin operated small stores inside the Ambassador and in Hollywood, but the Magnin family could no longer ignore the flourishing Wilshire Boulevard market. Hunt was allowed to make experimental use of brilliant white marble, with black-granite trim at sidewalk level. Details of the marble installation were so demanding that a scale model was built of plaster and kept nearby for consultation during construction. The result, according to one review, was a "symphony of beauty." In the rear, the auto court entrance rivaled Bullock's Wilshire in magnificence. Inside, I. Magnin specialized in couture fashions and fancy appointments, and developed a following as loyal as J.G. Bullock's partisans down the street.

Rivals became allies in 1944 when Bullock's bought out I. Magnin, acquiring the store at New Hampshire Avenue and another, also designed by Hunt, in Beverly Hills. The stores retained their separate identities through tumultuous ownership changes, but over time the customers of both began to age. Younger shoppers went elsewhere. Bullock's Wilshire, in particular, found its upscale, personalized service drawing fewer patrons, a trend worsened by the Wilshire district's socioeconomic decline in the 1970s and '80s. The store faced the same cultural forces that left the Ambassador a relic: as the Wilshire district had originally overtaken downtown, newer, more fashionable shopping malls were overtaking Wilshire. Fashion-conscious Los Angeles simply did not look to the close-in area of Wilshire anymore, not with newer, more popular stores like Saks Fifth Avenue and Neiman Marcus in Beverly Hills and in suburban malls. Bullock's Wilshire opened branches

Patrons could shop all day without carrying any bags. Purchases were delivered by "route boys" to the grand porte cochere off Wilshire Place, where departing customers would find everything loaded in their cars. The ceiling fresco "Spirit of Transportation" measures thirty-six by twenty-four feet.

in Palm Springs, Orange County and the San Fernando Valley, chasing after its upscale customers—and even removed the apostrophe from the name in a vain effort to freshen the brand's image.

Despite all the warning signs, it came as a blow to many longtime patrons when the Bullock's Wilshire name was struck from the celebrated store in 1990 and replaced by I. Magnin, in a desperate move to entice shoppers. Two years later, during the four days of rioting that swept Los Angeles after a suburban jury acquitted white police officers of beating black suspect Rodney King, looters broke into the store and shattered every display case on the first floor. Upper floors were spared only because fleeing staffers shut off the elevators—the original decision to build the store without escalators may have saved the landmark from ruin. At least three fires were set but didn't spread. Like the Robert Kennedy assassination did for the Ambassador, the riot spelled doom for the era of upscale shopping at 3050 Wilshire Boulevard.

As the inevitable end neared, long-vanished regulars returned to clean out the shoe departments and enjoy a final Bombay salad with iced tea. Two months after the Town House a block away shut its doors, the I. Magnin that to many was really Bullock's Wilshire in mufti closed as well—on April 13, 1993. Heartfelt eulogies filled the air. "I put the experience of shopping at Bullock's Wilshire—and the tearoom and the architecture and the salesladies there for forty years—in the same category as a summer evening at the Hollywood Bowl, a meal at Musso and Frank's, a ballgame at Dodger Stadium," television host Huell Howser told the *Times*. The paper's fashion editor, however, cautioned against the sentimentality. "Stores close because people don't shop in them. All the nostalgia in the world, for white-gloved elevator operators and tearooms filled with sweet-looking grannies, won't save a store. Shopping will." Los Angeles no longer wanted to shop in that part of Wilshire Boulevard.

Restoration of Bullock's Wilshire by Southwestern University School of Law and architect Ronald A. Altoon revived much of the building's original splendor. The famous tearoom, remodeled to the original desert theme, serves as the student lunchroom. Original clocks, artworks and details were incorporated into the law library and meeting rooms on the lower floors, and the exterior terra cotta and granite were gently cleaned of decades of dirt. The building is listed on the National Register of Historic Places. At night, floods of light again illuminate the tower so that it stands out for miles around, a call to remember what Wilshire Boulevard means to the city.

On the ceiling of the store's ground-breaking porte cochere, master muralist Anthony Heinsbergen, then seventy-eight years old, oversaw the careful restoration of a fresco secco by Rumanian artist Herman Sachs. It pays tribute to the modern age of transportation, and depicts Mercury, the winged Roman god of travel, surrounded by symbols of mobility current in 1929: an ocean liner, a Santa Fe Superchief locomotive, a Maddux Airlines plane, the *Graf Zeppelin* that had stopped in Los Angeles just months before. There is a curious omission, however. The mode of travel that made Bullock's Wilshire possible—the automobile—is not present.

Restoration of Bullock's Wilshire involved cleaning decades of grime off the tower's terra cotta and copper finish. The once-deluxe Town House on Lafayette Park was converted in 2001 to family apartments. Simon's sandwich stand in the foreground was located at the corner of Wilshire and Hoover Street.

CHAPTER FOUR

Wilshire Center

AT THE BOULEVARD'S intersection with Western Avenue, a mile closer to the ocean than the restored Bullock's Wilshire building, a busy subway station and the shadows cast by skyscraper towers create just the hint of a Manhattan vibe. Los Angeles is too spacious and car-centric to truly imitate a New York City street scene, but the imagery is appropriate to the corner. In the late 1920s, Wilshire at Western became, by local reckoning, the busiest traffic intersection in the country. Boosters touted Los Angeles's new main thoroughfare as the "Fifth Avenue of the West."

It was a hyperbolic slogan, repeated countless times at chamber of commerce luncheons and in promotional materials by the Wilshire Boulevard

Wilshire at Western Avenue became the traffic epicenter of Los Angeles in the late 1920s. Homes gave way to shopping centers like the McKinley Building, behind the double-decker bus, and its near-twin the Wilshire Central. Under construction in the distance is Wilshire Boulevard Temple's dome.

Association. But there was something behind it. A 1928 cartoon in the *Times* spoke for all of the believers when it depicted Wilshire and Western as the commercial crossroads of the future, with the boulevard encased in a solid canyon of office and store façades marching shoulder-to-shoulder to the horizon. Although Wilshire Boulevard never fully lived up to the Fifth Avenue hype, the district known as Wilshire Center—from Lafayette Park west to Wilton Place—did become the elite Los Angeles business address the boosters envisioned.

For about half the span of the twentieth century, corporate CEOs strove to be located in Mid-Wilshire, preferably in a tall building with their company's logo emblazoned across the top for the whole city to admire. A high-rent office suite with an address of 3000-something Wilshire Boulevard advertised a certain level of career success for surgeons, lawyers and other professionals. Richard Neutra, the celebrated Modernist architect, felt it was "one of his life's darkest disappointments that he never received a Wilshire Boulevard commission," according to biographer Thomas S. Hines.

Wilshire Center's variegated skyline of Art Deco-era towers, magnificent European-inspired churches and post-World War II high-rise boxes forms the most visually uproarious section along the entire boulevard, and one could argue in all of Los Angeles. Found there are the former corporate homes of Texaco and Getty Oil, numerous foreign consulates, perhaps the most beautiful Jewish temple in the country, and a large collection of Korean American shops and nightclubs. The boulevard's tallest building outside of downtown Los Angeles soars over Wilshire Center, on the site of the first Brown Derby. And on the southeast corner of Wilshire and Western stands an exemplary creation that in the Twenties stood for the uninhibited aspirations of the Fifth Avenue of the West boosters.

Stiles O. Clements was the right architect for the project, given what was riding on it. His stylish interpretations of the expansive era were appearing all along the boulevard and elsewhere in the city. At Wilshire and Western he conceived an exuberant design that elevated the intersection by its presence. The base filled the block back to Oxford Avenue and swallowed up the childhood home of actor Jackie Coogan. Display windows at the sidewalk repeated on the second story to entice riders on the open top deck of the public buses that serviced Wilshire. The crowning feature that brought astonished raves from the city's aesthetes was an alluring Zigzag Moderne tower, covered in custom-glazed aqua-green tiles that made the Pellissier Building appear to glow in the soft evening light of summer. Vertical lines and chevrons teased the eye to read more skyward thrust than actually was there. "Just twelve stories high but with enough apparent soar to entice King Kong," architect and critic Charles W. Moore wrote a half-century later.

Physicians and dentists quickly grabbed space on the upper floors. The ground level housed a movie theater that became regaled for its dazzling entry—a jazzy neon marquee, terrazzo floor and wild sculpted sunburst on the ceiling. G. Albert Lansburgh, a renowned creator of early movie palaces, designed the interior, with artwork by Anthony Heinsbergen, the Elks Lodge muralist. The Warner Bros. Western opened October 7, 1931 with a gala premiere attended by the mayor and so many Hollywood stars that a temporary footbridge arched above Wilshire to separate the glitterati from traffic. The theater shut down during the Depression, then reopened later as the Wil-Tern (named for the intersection.) Later owners streamlined the name to the Wiltern. When plans by Franklin Life Insurance to demolish the building were revealed in 1979, the Los Angeles Conservancy and the preservation community mobilized. The building was listed on the National Register of Historic Places and, ultimately, developer Wayne Ratkovich and architect Brenda Levin saved and restored the Pellissier and Wiltern.

Back in 1928, when the *Times* declared the corner "The World's Heaviest Traveled Intersection," the news helped clarify the obvious. Wilshire Boulevard, by then paved from Westlake Park to the ocean, had become the principal east-west route in pre-freeway Los Angeles. It was the conduit from the past, represented by downtown, to the future hopes reflected in Westside developments such as the Miracle Mile and the new University of California campus in the hills above Westwood. Western Avenue, too, fulfilled a purpose as the busiest cross street between downtown and the Pacific.

Not long before, civic leaders had vigorously disagreed about the future role of Wilshire Boulevard. Speculators and real estate men foresaw a street bustling with commerce—stores like Bullock's Wilshire, hotels and office buildings. A leading

From his office on the southeast corner, Henry de Roulet shared the booster vision of a mini-downtown around Wilshire and Western. First would have to come crosswalks and white lines between lanes.

proponent of this was Henry de Roulet, who sold lots in his family's tract from a wood-frame house on the southeast corner of Wilshire and Western. His grandfather, a French-born sheepherder named Germaine Pellissier, had bought one hundred forty acres from the Southern Pacific Railroad in 1882, more than a dozen years before Wilshire Boulevard was even a line in the soil. Perhaps he sensed something about the future direction of Los Angeles that others did not. As the city crept west, the family subdivided plots in what they called Pellissier Square, at Wilshire and Western. It was de Roulet who would later commission Clements to build a stirring tower at the corner; the distinctive color of the ceramic tiles is Pellissier Green.

The competing vision beheld Wilshire not as a business address but as a picturesque scenic drive sweeping all the way to the sea, graced with beautiful gardens and mansions. Henry O'Melveny's mansion stood at 3250 Wilshire Boulevard and he gave eloquent speeches extolling his idea of the grandest processional in the West, a rival of the Avenue du Bois de Boulogne in Paris. His allies included downtown interests which feared, rightly, that commercial development on Wilshire would draw customers away from the traditional business district. Their garden parkway, pitched relentlessly under the auspices of the Community Development Association, defied the city's inexorable tug toward the coast and failed some reality checks. O'Melveny's pleasure drive would pass beside unsightly oil derricks and the smelly, bubbling pools of the La Brea tar pits. It

Klieg lights and a brass band enlivened opening night on October 7, 1931, at the Warner Bros. Western theater. Stars arrived via temporary footbridge over Wilshire to see *Alexander Hamilton,* starring George Arliss. The landmark theater later was renamed the Wiltern.

would need the cooperation of Beverly Hills and Santa Monica, separate cities along the proposed route that already resisted pressure to join Los Angeles in its imperial ambitions.

The old pueblo's evolution into a city of drivers, however, posed the more insurmountable impediment. The *Los Angeles Record* observed as early as 1920, "Twenty years ago influential people rode in streetcars. Today they ride in automobiles." Use of the Pacific Electric Red Cars and inter-urban

Early Wilshire bus commuters could enjoy the fresh air or stay down below. Talk of an elevated monorail through Wilshire Center in the 1960s sparked passionate objections. Even after the Red Line subway reached Western in the 1990s, the boulevard remained the city's busiest bus corridor.

trains peaked in 1924, then declined even as the population doubled. Traffic congestion downtown reached crisis levels as more motor vehicles tried to squeeze through the narrow nineteenth-century streets each day than were registered in all of New York state.

In something of a panic, elected city officials asked an influential board of outside experts, led by landscape architect Frederick Law Olmsted Jr. and St. Louis urban planner Harland Bartholomew, to propose a way out of the mess. Their Major Traffic Street Plan for Los Angeles smacked the citizenry in the face. "The . . . congestion problem of Los Angeles is exceeded by that of no other city," Olmsted and Bartholomew began. They recommended the entire system be rethought, with selected residential streets widened into major boulevards spaced a mile apart. Wilshire received special attention, but not the sort that O'Melveny desired. The report pointedly rejected his parkway to the sea as a squandering of future potential.

Instead, Olmsted and Bartholomew urged that Wilshire be elevated to elite status, toward the ocean and east through downtown, forming a cross-town highway to the Boyle Heights district. The concept recalled Charles Mulford Robinson's call in 1907 for Wilshire to be a thoroughfare of uncommon destiny. Olmsted and Bartholomew saw in Wilshire a splendid civic opportunity to fashion a boulevard that would not only carry traffic, but also be "notably handsome and artistically impressive." Great boulevards have one dominant element, they argued: on Wilshire the drama should come from a broad pavement with clear views of architecturally striking structures, as on Avenue des Champs-Elysees in Paris. Gardens would only get in the way.

Voters embraced the Olmsted-Bartholomew

vision by a five-to-one margin. Crews soon began to straighten, level and expand Wilshire into a modern blacktop boulevard—with concrete curbs and sidewalks, lined with palm trees—stretching five miles from Westlake Park out to Fairfax Avenue. "One of the largest paving jobs in the history of Los Angeles," the *Times* boasted upon completion in 1927. At the end of a vituperative election campaign, voters also rezoned the twenty-five blocks from the park to Western Avenue for commercial use. New stores, banks and cafés quickly opened. Work began on Bullock's Wilshire and the Pellissier tower at Western Avenue. On February 8, 1928, thousands of onlookers cheered as Mayor George Cryer threw a switch that illuminated five miles of boulevard with custom-built Wilshire Special lamps. They were gigantic, the most distinctive in Los Angeles, with a massive rectangular light box that incorporated four stylized female figures. Brightly lit and uncommonly wide, Wilshire Boulevard stood apart from other mere streets.

Even so, the boulevard of destiny did not reach downtown, which remained the pulsing center of the city. Wilshire stopped at Westlake Park, dumping its traffic onto local streets. To get downtown, drivers had to line up and turn in front of the old Otis mansion at Park View Street, then complete the last mile and a half squeezing past the streetcars on Sixth and Seventh. A partial solution, obvious to some, presented itself in Orange Street, a residential avenue that climbed the hills of Orange Heights between Westlake Park and downtown. It was narrow and steep, but lined up just right with Wilshire Boulevard—between Sixth and Seventh.

For old-timers on Orange Street, it sounded all too familiar. In 1908 the city council had gazed into the future and renamed their little street

Wilshire Boulevard. Three weeks later, though, the council recanted. Both sides had disliked the name change. Mansion-dwellers in General Otis's neighborhood complained that applying the Wilshire name to such an ordinary avenue besmirched the boulevard's image. Orange Street residents, in turn, sniffed: "We are not the kind of snobs who would call our back alleys *boulevards*. We intend to tell inquiring strangers that Wilshire Boulevard is only an extension of Orange Street."

In the 1920s, however, there was no stopping the Wilshire juggernaut. Road crews invaded with sledgehammers and graders to widen Orange Street, razing whatever stood in the way. The Rex Arms—a luxurious residence in its day, praised in 1913 as the "final word in apartment-house construction"—escaped demolition only by shaving off the front of the structure and making do with fewer rooms. The surgery was more difficult than it sounds, since the Rex Arms stood eight stories tall.

Wilshire's eclectic blend of architecture was established early. Stiles Clements gave the McKinley Building a Churrigueresque flavor, then in the same decade embraced Zigzag Moderne for his milestone Pellissier Building. The tower's distinctive color is officially "Pellissier Green."

Eventually, though, Wilshire Boulevard ambitions hit an immovable wall.

The problem was that Orange Street ended at Figueroa Street, on the edge of downtown. From there, Wilshire would have to bludgeon through twenty-one blocks of existing stores, hotels and homes to reach the Los Angeles River and cross to the Eastside. Inflicting that kind of carnage required more political will than city leaders could summon. Officials halted Wilshire's eastward push into downtown after four blocks, at Grand Avenue. Once that work was finished, only a short quarter-mile gap remained to complete Wilshire Boulevard's route to the sea, but it was the most painful breach to close. The gap was bucolic Westlake Park, where it all began in 1895. Drivers in both directions still had to jog around the park to continue on Wilshire Boulevard.

A tunnel under the park or a bridge over it were considered but rejected. Political squabbling delayed work for several years, but finally the state supreme court allowed construction of a curving viaduct through the park. Part of the lake plus lawns and walking paths were sacrificed. On December 7, 1934, Mayor Frank Shaw cut the ribbon and declared Wilshire Boulevard "California's most famous thoroughfare." Wilshire was free to play its lead role in the Los Angeles story, a boulevard created for the new breed of Angeleno who drove everywhere.

WHERE DOWNTOWN STILL CLUNG to the past, Wilshire Boulevard represented the future as it would be shaped by the automobile. There was no timidity about embracing the Automobile Age, the good and the less desirable. Just as the display windows at Bullock's Wilshire targeted passing motorists, billboards attempted to entice them to buy everything from liquor to laundry soap. A hundred signs mounted on sturdy scaffolding popped up, angled toward oncoming traffic. Typically they were dressed up with flowerbeds or well-kept lawns and lit with floodlights, turning a drive along Wilshire into one long advertisement.

Wilshire also functioned as a laboratory where Los Angeles worked out the terms of its devotion to driving. As early as 1909, the city streets inspector used the boulevard to test the best method of reducing road dust: he sprinkled heavy oil over the dirt surface on the south half, lighter oil on the north side. In 1922, after a rash of collisions at Wilshire and Western, drivers were surprised to find a circle of concrete, forty feet in diameter, placed in the center of the intersection. *Touring Topics,* the magazine of the Automobile Club of Southern California, dubbed the structure Traffic's Magic Circle and explained to members how it worked:

> *"If all drivers wishing to make a right-hand turn would work towards the right as they approach and those desiring to turn to the left get to that side of the traffic, leaving the center lane for those who wish to go straight ahead, there will be no congestion."*

Since Wilshire's pavement was unusually wide, engineers in 1929 painted on white-lacquer stripes to divide lanes. Until then, streets had been devoid of markings and drivers just followed the oil drip lines—but discipline would break down at busy intersections. Synchronized traffic signals were introduced in 1931 from Westlake Park to Beverly Hills. They allowed drivers to sail along at twenty-five miles an hour without stopping, the "most pronounced

EAST OF MACARTHUR PARK

Wilshire Boulevard never became the prestige address downtown that it did on the Westside. On maps, it resembles a dagger plunged between Sixth and Seventh streets, more intruder than civic treasure. Wilshire's four-block penetration into downtown is not without distinctive buildings, however.

Thirty stories above the T-intersection at Grand Avenue where the boulevard ends, Bunyanesque letters shout One Wilshire from a white marble façade. Over Wilshire and Hope Street, the boulevard's most prominent office tower soars sixty-two stories. Once the West's tallest skyscraper, Aon Center was built without fire sprinklers. That proved to be a fatal oversight in 1988 when flames erupted on the twelfth floor and climbed toward night workers trapped above. Firefighters saved all but one life, but their chief later admitted he feared the building was lost. Los Angeles high-rises now come with sprinklers.

At Flower Street the tasteful Pegasus apartments are regarded by fans of architect Welton Becket as a Late Moderne gem. Sleek terra cotta with Art Deco touches, it was the head-quarters of General Petroleum, parent corporation of Mobil gas stations. The Pegasus name comes from Mobil's blood-red, winged-horse logo.

At Figueroa Street, the hotel on the southwest corner dates from the early 1950s, when it was the ultra-modern Statler Center. The fifty-two-story, bullet-shaped tower on the northwest corner rose in the late 1980s on the site of St. Paul's Episcopal Cathedral.

West beyond the Harbor Freeway, Good Samaritan Hospital existed when its stretch of Wilshire was still called Orange Street. Same for the converted circa-1905 home at Wilshire and Witmer Street. It once belonged to Charles Chapman, developer of the Chapman Park market and hotel, but someone mistook it for the home of Charlie Chaplin and filled the walls of the restaurant now there with pictures of the actor. And the blue façade at 1648 Wilshire was the Depression-era home and studio of the much-admired movie theater designer and architect S. Charles Lee. Its design resembles his landmark Max Factor building in Hollywood.

Covey's U-Drive just missed being demolished to make way for the boulevard's 1920s extension into downtown. Instead, Covey's received a prime location on the newly created southeast corner of Wilshire and Figueroa Street—but the price stayed at three dollars per day.

improvement made in Los Angeles traffic regulation in many years," the chief of the Traffic Association said. These too required adjustment. Drivers were used to mechanical semaphore arms that swung up and down and read "STOP" and "GO." The first signal lights also produced an audible gong to alert drivers and pedestrians. The sounds prompted widespread objection, however, and were shut off.

Cars needed gasoline, of course, and eventually more than one hundred service stations would cover the boulevard from end to end. The first dispenser, opened in 1909, was a tank hung on the back of Earl Gilmore's horse-drawn wagon parked at La Brea Avenue. The most stylish early station debuted just west of Vermont in 1927. At the California Petroleum Super Station's grand opening, an orchestra played and film stars Buster Keaton and the Talmadge sisters put in appearances. Calpet Girls in Tunisian costumes greeted customers, and male station attendants pumped gas in white shirts, bow ties and maroon jackets with puttees and breeches. The

Fashion and attentive service merged at the California Petroleum Super Station. It was stylish enough to satisfy the demanding shoppers at nearby Bullock's Wilshire and inspire a photo montage, complete with posed Calpet Girls. An office building erected on the site houses the Republic of South Korea consulate.

station's design included a Moorish-domed cashier hall and a ladies' lounge furnished tastefully with Venetian mirrors, cozy rockers and settees. Calpet appealed to the sort of motorists who wished to be well taken care of and who nurtured and loved their cars.

These were the same select customers who bought Packards from Earle C. Anthony and exclusive Auburn-Cords and Duesenbergs from the ostentatious dealership built in 1932 by E.L. Cord, at the northwest corner of Wilshire and Mariposa. Cord had migrated to Los Angeles from Auburn, Indiana, after taking over the presidency of the Auburn–Fuller Co., a maker of fine custom-built automobiles with innovative hideaway headlights and bucket seats. Albert C. Martin, a prominent architect involved in erecting City Hall, designed Cord's Art Deco headquarters. Cord himself outfitted the opulent showroom with a polished-marble floor, hardwood finishes, thirty-foot ceilings and dramatic display windows. Upstairs were four floors of service departments, the company offices and Cord's radio stations, KFAC and KFVD, which had their transmission towers on the roof. At different times, he also owned Checker Cab, the predecessor to American Airlines and valuable land along Wilshire Boulevard in Beverly Hills.

By the time Cord came along, Wilshire Boulevard was the logical place to build an eye-pleasing edifice. The Pellissier Building's green terra cotta tower had just opened. Mid-Wilshire was also known for its architecturally dramatic churches and

Industrialist Errett Lobban Cord's showroom brought luxury Auburn-Cords and Duesenbergs to the Depression-era boulevard. KFAC, the city's first all-classical radio station, remained after the upstairs service bays were converted to offices in 1951. The consulate of Indonesia took over the building, which adjoins Wilshire Christian Church.

synagogues, geared at mobile Angelenos and built to last on a generous scale. Many of the institutions became the city's most influential and upscale houses of worship. Membership typically numbered in the thousands, the pews filled with mayors, judges, publishers and other Los Angeles movers. Congregations didn't advertise their addresses, just their corners: Wilshire at Berendo for Immanuel Presbyterian, Wilshire at Harvard for St. Basil's Catholic Church, Wilshire at St. Andrews for St.

James' Episcopal. They formed a boulevard community that crossed denomination lines. During the years around World War II, the churches all joined for an annual Easter procession. Neighbors also took care of one another. Wilshire Boulevard Temple welcomed offers to hold High Holy Days services in the larger, Gothic sanctuary at Immanuel Presbyterian, a few blocks east. Likewise, when the original St. Basil's burned down, Wilshire Boulevard Temple opened its sanctuary to displaced parishioners. At the dedication of a new St. Basil's, in 1969, Rabbi Edgar F. Magnin was an honored guest alongside James Francis Cardinal McIntyre.

Once Wilshire Christian Church graced the corner at Normandie Avenue in 1923, religious architecture on the boulevard began to aspire. Wilshire Center became the home of "million-dollar churches." Looking east, the tall building beyond the original Brown Derby is the Gaylord Hotel.

The destroyed St. Basil's had been designed by architect Albert C. Martin in 1920 at Catalina and Seventh Street and four years later was sectioned and moved to Wilshire. A.C. Martin & Associates designed the new St. Basil's, which includes impressive 177-foot-high stained glass windows and bronze doors by Los Angeles sculptor Claire Falkenstein. The first grand religious edifice in the neighborhood had been Wilshire Christian Church, built on land donated by the Chapman Park developers. Designed in a Romanesque style in 1923 by Robert H. Orr, a prominent architect of Protestant churches, it has remained a visually striking landmark at the corner of Wilshire and Normandie. The rose window above the west-facing entrance is the church's pride. Executed by the respected Judson Studios, the window is said to be a copy of one in the Rheims Cathedral in France. The poured-concrete exterior finish reveals the ridges left by the original wood forms, a feature also found at the immense First Congregational Church that faces onto Lafayette Park.

Immanuel Presbyterian is the most Gothic-looking structure found anywhere on Wilshire. Dark and brooding with a 205-foot bell tower, some of its windows also are from the Judson Studios. Moving to the boulevard had been controversial within the congregation. Some members opposed the idea of giving up a prestige downtown location to start over as a "country church," but the impressive design by Chauncey F. Skilling, a leader in the church and a former city councilman, assuaged those concerns. Immanuel grew into one of the largest congregations on the boulevard, peaking at more than forty-five hundred members. St. James' Episcopal, also with Judson windows, is a Flemish Gothic Revival gem built on the site of a Craftsman-style home that was converted to

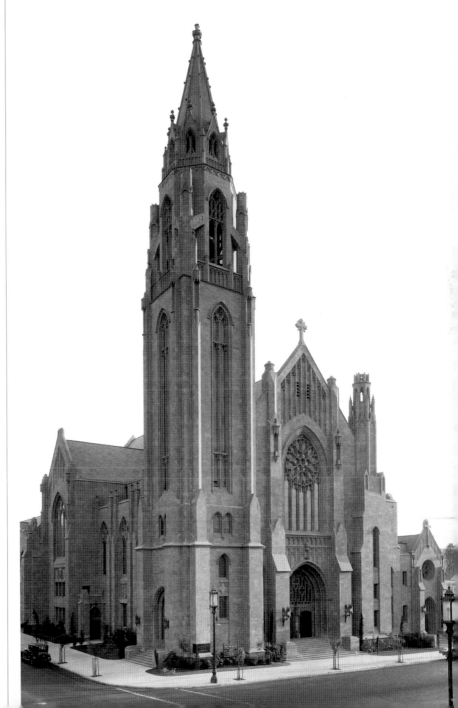

Immanuel Presbyterian, a towering gothic presence since 1929, seats two thousand worshippers. But since membership has dipped along the boulevard, some of the classic churches retain Hollywood location agents to rent their sanctuaries for filming.

One month after the dedication of Immanuel Presbyterian, Wilshire Boulevard Temple opened to glowing reviews. Stone steps and superb doors fashioned from East Indian teakwood present a dignified face to the street, but the dome is what people remember.

church use and moved to Wilshire in 1920. Frank Sinatra, Duke Ellington and other musical legends attended the 1965 funeral of Nat King Cole at St. James'. It contains the organ that once delighted worshippers at St. Paul's Episcopal Cathedral, located at Wilshire and Figueroa until being razed in 1980 for a fifty-two-story office building.

The only Wilshire religious institution honored with inclusion on the National Register of Historic Places is the domed Wilshire Boulevard Temple at Hobart Boulevard. Congregation B'nai B'rith, established in 1862, had been the oldest downtown Jewish synagogue when the members voted to relocate on Wilshire. At the dedication in 1929, banker

Many of Los Angeles' most respected Jewish leaders helped to build the Wilshire temple. It became the spiritual home of the community and elevated the boulevard's stature.

Henry de Roulet's aspirations for an urban boulevard came true. Wilshire's route west from the city's old center functioned as a new form of American downtown—linear yet vertical, the spine at the core of a modern metropolis.

Marco Hellman presented the ark, and Jack Warner, one of the studio-owning Warner brothers, bestowed murals depicting the history of the Hebrew people painted by Hugo Ballin. The artist, whose work also decorates Griffith Observatory, painted on canvas in his Santa Monica studio, then mounted the murals around the hundred-foot-high, mosaic-inlaid dome that vaults above the octagonal sanctuary. Such prominent art was atypical in synagogues. But Rabbi Magnin—a relation of the I. Magnin department store family—hoped it would add warmth and an element of mysticism. The temple's architecture by David Allison and Abraham Edelman is regarded as a work of art in itself. It features Italian and Belgian marble, carved mahogany and inlaid gold.

WILSHIRE'S SANCTUARIES welcomed neighbors, but they catered to worshippers who arrived by car. Likewise, drive-in markets and cafés were logical extensions of the new mobile ethos. At the time they began appearing on Wilshire and other Los Angeles thoroughfares, neither were common elsewhere in the United States. Harry Carpenter's Sandwich Stand was the first of the notable drive-in coffee shops, opened in 1931 at the southwest corner of Wilshire and Western. It served burgers and coffee in a brilliantly lit octagonal dining room open twenty-four hours a day.

The idea of driving right up to the door for a quick bite—or better yet, staying in your car and ordering from an attendant—caught on quickly among the new Angelenos. Carpenter's added another shop at Wilshire and Vermont, opposite the rival Roberts Brothers stand, which grabbed the southwest corner. Drive-ins of the day often served harder stuff in adjoining cocktail lounges, such as the Starlite Room at the Melody Lane, which took over the Carpenter's location at Western. Many Wilshire drive-ins, such as Truman's in Westwood and Dolores in Beverly Hills, became beloved hangouts and, in their passing, the objects of much nostalgia over roller-skating carhops and Friday night dates.

Unlike the demise of favorite burger joints, the closing of the small drive-in markets on Wilshire and other boulevards in Los Angeles evoked less fawning. Their prevalence in the late 1920s, however, had been an important marker of the emerging auto culture: they demonstrated the preference of residents in the new Westside neighborhoods to shop near home and run errands by car. Taking notice, Ralphs and other supermarket chains hired prominent commercial architects such as Stiles Clements to design eye-grabbing stores. Stylish architecture was high on the agenda of the Wilshire Boulevard Association, based on the theory that attractive design would be helpful in drawing shoppers.

In the 1920s and '30s, this led to an emphasis on Art Deco and other modern designs. Wilshire's early stores and office buildings were sunny and spacious for the times, in contrast to the drab Midwestern feel of places like Hollywood Boulevard, Wilshire's chief competition for the loyalty of downtown expatriates. Wilshire Center, wrote historian Richard Longstreth, was a "motor-age Champs-Elysees, punctuated by office towers soaring between

Angelenos loved their cars, so drive-ins just made sense. They stayed open twenty-four hours and introduced the stylish carhop. Most cafés were round or octagonal and featured a lighted Art Deco pylon to attract drivers. Some, like Melody Lane at Wilshire and Western, served cocktails along with traditional fare.

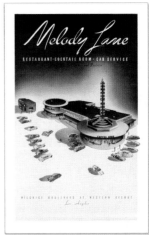

elegant little stores that paid homage to tradition and to current haute-monde tastes."

The thirteen-story Wilshire Professional building, at the corner of Wilshire and St. Andrews Place, was a good example. Its Zigzag Moderne tower shrinks in girth as it rises, the step-back ensuring that should another tall building go up next door, the two would not intrude on each other's air and light. The look repeated itself several places along the boulevard.

Besides Art Deco, Clements's firm contributed the best local interpretations of the Churrigueresque style, a strain of Spanish Revival popular in Southern California after the 1915 Panama exhibition at Balboa Park in San Diego. Elaborate and sometimes fantastic ornamentation defines the style. A fine surviving example stands at the northeast corner of Wilshire and Berendo, opposite the Talmadge apartments. Maidens and gleeful monkeys hide in the sculpted flourishes that decorate the doorways and windows. The building, erected as commercial art studios, housed decorators and the French American School of Costume Designing, among other businesses.

Another Clements contribution to Wilshire Center's personality sat at the corner of Wilshire and Oxford Avenue, opposite his Pellissier tower. The McKinley Building, designed in 1923, impressed aficionados with its Spanish Revival flourishes, roof tiles in varying red shades, playful wrought-iron details and a charming, secretive inner plaza. "The shopper feels that he is in another small world," the journal *Pacific Coast Architect* gushed in the 1920s. Deemed eligible for the National Register of Historic Places but never officially designated, the McKinley was demolished in 1998 after incurring damage from earthquakes and subway excavation. The Red Line subway follows Wilshire Boulevard for two miles from Westlake Park to Western Avenue, then turns north toward Hollywood and the San Fernando Valley.

Perhaps the best preserved of Clements's Spanish-influenced work in Wilshire Center is Chapman Plaza, located a block off the boulevard at Sixth Street and Alexandria Avenue. It opened in 1929 as the innovative drive-in Chapman Park Market. Bigger and more ambitious than the markets on Wilshire, it resembles a fortress, with thick sandstone-textured concrete walls and erupting corner towers. Drivers enter an inner courtyard through a Spanish Revival archway. The market and its companion Chapman Park studio building across Alexandria, together with the old Chapman Park Hotel, formed a coherent complex of aesthetically pleasing commercial buildings. After the hotel was razed in the late 1960s for the Equitable Plaza skyscraper, the complex suffered. In the 1980s, however, preservationist Douglas Curran almost single-handedly restored the studio building. Wayne Ratkovich and Brenda Levin, after restoring the Pellissier Building, revived the market. Both Chapman Plaza and the studio building are city Historic–Cultural Monuments.

Wilshire Center's commercial heyday continued into the 1970s. After World War II, Los Angeles exploded in population and importance, and the boulevard attracted insurance firms, oil companies and other Fortune 500 corporations. Origins of the postwar high-rise cluster near Wilshire and Western can be traced in some fashion to a prominent New York real estate developer who discovered the boulevard by fluke. Traveling to Palm Springs in 1950, Norman Tishman stayed overnight at the Ambassador. "I looked out my window and saw a golf driving range. It seemed a waste of space," he told an interviewer. After his vacation, he returned and bought an entire block west of the Ambassador. Tishmanville, as *Los Angeles* magazine dubbed it, took form as three matching twelve-story glass boxes (at 3340, 3350 and 3360 Wilshire Boulevard) designed by Claude Beelman, the Elks Lodge architect. Before the decade was over, Tishman Realty and Construction had erected the five tallest office towers in Wilshire Center. When the city of Los Angeles began in 1957 to loosen height limits that had restricted most offices to one hundred fifty feet or thirteen stories, Tishman and other developers reached for the sky, building skyscrapers for their corporate clients.

Architects coveted these high-rise commissions in Wilshire Center and many, including Welton Becket, kept their offices there. In the postwar decades, Becket's firm designed offices for U.S. Borax and Travelers Insurance, Pierce National Life, and the tallest structure on Wilshire outside of downtown, the thirty-four-story former Equitable Life

Female athletes at the 1932 Olympics stayed in the original multistory hotel at Sixth and Alexandria. Soon after, gardens and Spanish-style bungalows filled the block where the first Brown Derby had been located. The Zephyr Room took over a converted wedding chapel.

PRIVATE SWIMMING POOL

CHAPMAN PARK HOTEL

The CHAPMAN PARK HOTEL and Bungalows

3401 WILSHIRE BLVD. LOS ANGELES 5, CALIF.

Zephyr Room WHERE YOU MEET THE STARS

ON FASHIONABLE WILSHIRE BOULEVARD

YOUR HOME IN A CALIFORNIA GARDEN

headquarters. Finished in 1969, the year Becket died, the Equitable tower was his twenty-fifth major undertaking on the boulevard.

By the 1980s, Wilshire Center's role had begun to change as Los Angeles-based corporate headquarters vanished through mergers or left the boulevard. On many blocks the predominant culture, both social and financial, became Korean American. The Republic of South Korea consulate occupies the site of the Calpet Super Station near Vermont Avenue. Texaco Oil's vacated headquarters became Korea Center, and the all-marble showcase store that I. Magnin abandoned after the 1992 riots became the Korean-oriented Wilshire Galleria. Infusions of capital from Korean corporations and investors revived Wilshire Center's status as an office district after the riots, when looting and firebombing marauders targeted Korean-owned establishments on Wilshire and elsewhere. Koreans still refer to the violence as *sa-ee-gu,* Korean for "4/29," the date the riots began. So many companies moved their offices out of Wilshire Center in the aftermath that historian Mike Davis called the area a "modern high-rise ghost town." Since then, smaller law firms and companies that cannot afford the high rents in newer high-rise areas such as Century City and Westwood have adopted Wilshire Center.

Koreatown, which sprawls in both directions from Wilshire Boulevard, has become a thriving center of commerce and nightlife. In upscale clubs, young, often-affluent Korean Americans gather to

Stiles Clements's fortress-like Chapman Park Market set the standard for drive-up establishments. Shoppers lured off Wilshire, a block away, parked in a secluded court and bought from their choice of grocers. The restored market is popular with young Korean Americans.

102

Developers hoped Wilshire would grow into a mini-Manhattan. That dream fell short, but company logos cluttered the 1950s skyline. In the foreground are Wilshire Christian Church, the Chapman Park Hotel.

drink and dance. More proof that the community has put the 1992 disturbance behind is Aroma Center, a retail complex that brought a bold new personality to the block between Hobart and Serrano Avenues. Offerings include a luxurious family health club, an international food court, a Starbucks coffee outlet and the city's most dramatic urban golf-driving range. Patrons at the fifth-floor Aroma Golf Academy enjoy a gorgeous view over the Wilshire district and hit into a giant net suspended above a parking garage. Aroma Center's most impressive contribution to the Wilshire streetscape, however, is a mammoth video screen, twenty-two feet tall by thirty-three feet wide, hung on the west wall. It plays twenty-first-century advertising in full color to motorists on the Automobile Age boulevard.

The former Equitable Life tower opened in 1969 on the site of the original Brown Derby and Chapman Park Hotel. It's now the tallest building in Koreatown.

CHAPTER FIVE

Park Mile

AT A SPOT three-and-a-half miles into the cacophony of Wilshire's westward path, something gives. At Wilton Place the boulevard of ambition goes mostly quiet. No more skyscrapers, subway stations or restaurants, just some landscaped office complexes and weed-choked vacant fields—the first of those since downtown—pushing against the Wilshire sidewalk. A lonely 1950s motel clashes like an intruder from a faraway place.

Officially known as Park Mile, this leg of Wilshire Boulevard has also been called the Dead Mile. If Henry O'Melveny's 1920s dream of a residential parkway survives anywhere, it is here. No stately mansions front on Wilshire anymore, but

Ladies who belonged to the Ebell of Los Angeles demanded uplifting luncheon speakers, good deeds and impeccable taste. When the club burned the mortgage on its Wilshire edifice, the governor, the mayor and the president of the bank dutifully attended.

plenty of them lurk just off the boulevard on the leafy avenues of the Fremont Place, Windsor Square and Hancock Park neighborhoods. Power brokers, society stalwarts and two *Los Angeles Times* publishers named Chandler—descendants of Harrison Gray Otis—have resided in these substantial homes, along with Hollywood celebrities and diplomats. The mayor's ceremonial residence, Getty House, occupies the corner of Sixth Street and Irving, one block off of Wilshire. Other renowned homes, including O'Melveny's, were moved here after originally facing onto Wilshire Boulevard.

Park Mile's low-key demeanor is a perk won through the years by some of the most politically connected homeowners in the city. Most people dislike skyscrapers looming over their backyards, but the residents who straddle Park Mile have traditionally possessed the clout to do something about it. Only a solitary Wilshire office tower casts its shadow on homes, and it is a quirk of the past constructed after years of legal skirmishing on the site of a mansion that appeared in the films *Sunset Blvd.* and *Rebel Without a Cause.*

Park Mile's intentionally low profile nonetheless reveals an impressive bunch of clues to the boulevard's history as Los Angeles's grand concourse. The 1920s Los Altos apartments, where Hearst and Davies slept over in quarters

designed by Julia Morgan, is entered on the National Register of Historic Places. A Hollywood talent agency occupies the last converted mansion that still looks over the boulevard. Also there is the former site of Perino's, once the unofficial clubhouse for the swells of Fremont Place and Hancock Park, and the corner where a Creek oil millionaire became famous as the "nation's richest Indian."

The residential streets off Park Mile were some of the grandest to be developed along the young boulevard. Windsor Square and Fremont Place were each subdivided in 1911, facing each other across the former *El Camino Viejo,* which divided *Rancho La Brea* on the north side from *Rancho las Cienegas* on the south. At the time, Wilshire Boulevard so far west of Los Angeles was a bumpy country drive. Those who motored out through the tumbleweeds and bean fields often were curious about the adobes they saw and the colorful rancho past.

Rancho La Brea was one of the most propitious land grants made in the Mexican era before

Much of Wilshire's route through the old Mexican ranchos west of town remained unpaved in 1916, but enough cars came by to attract billboards. Los Angeles High School was under construction on the Avila and Rimpau families' former *Rancho las Cienegas.*

Windsor Square, Los Angeles, Cal.

After fields of wheat, oats and barley were transformed into English gardens, the *Times* in 1914 called Windsor Square "fashionable."

California gained statehood in 1850—a square league, 4,439 acres, given by the *alcalde* of Los Angeles to a lucky man. Antonio José Rocha had landed in Alta California poor and soaked, a Portuguese ship jumper who talked his way out of being deported. It was the practice of the Mexican authorities to bequeath sections of land in the sparsely populated province to homesteaders who committed to raise crops and build an adobe. Rocha's grant did not seem especially valuable at the time—it included the hazardous communal *brea* pits, where citizens gathering tar could not help but notice the many bones of strange-looking animals that had become trapped.

Away from the tar seeps, though, the terrain was fertile. A good seasonal stream, *El Arroyo del Jardin de las Flores,* flowed down out of the hills. A decade after California joined the Union, Rocha's family sold the rancho to Henry Hancock. His widow got the money for her magnificent Villa Madonna at Wilshire and Vermont by selling off pieces of the

rancho. One large tract became the original settlement of Hollywood. Windsor Square sprouted on a plot of two hundred acres that Mrs. Hancock sold for four hundred dollars an acre along the rutted *camino* to Los Angeles that would become Wilshire Boulevard. The investors who bought it held on through several real estate cycles and finally got five thousand dollars an acre in 1911. R.A. Rowan, the developer who took over the land, used the newspapers to spread the word about his Windsor Square tract. "The entire area is high and sightly, commanding an unsurpassed view of the mountains, the ocean front and the rest of the city," the *Times* reported.

Hoping to evoke the verdant grace of an English residential park, Rowan planted shade trees and encouraged homeowners to landscape lavishly but not erect fences. He wanted Windsor Square to surpass Chester Square, located near the University of Southern California, as the city's most dignified district. Utility lines were buried out of sight. Distinctive three-headed street lamps bore the Windsor Square crest. A *Times* article soon featured the "palatial new homes" of Windsor Square. The community grew to include more than eleven hundred residences and form what the Los Angeles Conservancy calls one of

Residents can tell Hancock Park from Windsor Square, but casual visitors just see streets lined with mansions of the rich and sometimes famous. Sunshine Hall, center, and Los Tiempos, right, are on South Lorraine Avenue. The Petitfils home on Plymouth includes ceiling murals painted by Anthony Heinsbergen.

the largest collections of period revival homes in the county, between Van Ness Avenue and Arden Boulevard. The two-story Italian Renaissance home at Sixth and Lorraine, built in 1921 from a design by architect Charles F. Plummer, had original ceiling murals by Anthony Heinsbergen. Sunshine Hall at 419 S. Lorraine is designated a city Historic–Cultural Monument. Another official landmark, at 637 S. Lucerne, is the graceful 1899 Higgins mansion designed by John C. Austin that was cut up and moved by truck in 1923 from Wilshire and Rampart.

Windsor Square's early competition lay just across Wilshire to the south, clearly visible over the open fields. Fremont Place sprouted on a rise of fifty acres culled from the former *Rancho las Cienegas,* a marshy sprawl long enjoyed by hunters. "In one morning's shoot on the Cienega, H.M. Mitchell and myself killed eighty-seven jack-snipes," lawyer J.A.

Graves, a partner of O'Melveny's, once wrote. Like Windsor Square, Fremont Place was sold as a park-like refuge of sedate mansions. Impressive cast-concrete gates designed by architect Martyn Haenke marked the entrance on Wilshire Boulevard. Weekend pleasure drivers exploring the new route toward the sea would not miss the point that Fremont Place was meant to be no ordinary subdivision.

Austin designed the first mansion at 55 Fremont Place for Oklahoma oil millionaire Martin H. Mosier. Italian Renaissance in style, it commanded a hill facing east, toward the city. Spectacular and solid, with a mahogany-finished interior, the Mosier mansion—like many homes in Fremont Place and Windsor Square—has passed down through a succession of owners. The Reverend James Fifield Jr., outspoken minister of the First Congregational Church at Lafayette Park in the middle of the century, also

Architect Martyn Haenke's concrete entrance gates for Fremont Place have commanded respect since 1911. They still exist, unlike the three-headed street lamps bearing the Windsor Square crest.

lived at number 55. The wife of heavyweight boxer Muhammad Ali oversaw a thorough restoration when they resided there in the late 1970s. The home to its rear, at 100 Fremont Place, was commissioned by King Gillette, heir to the Gillette razor fortune, in the style of a Honolulu hotel, with costly island coconut palms brought in to complete the look. It was later the residence of James Francis Cardinal McIntyre, leader of the Roman Catholic Archdiocese in Los Angeles, who added a chapel. A stand of Hawaiian sugarcane grows in the backyard.

In the first edition of *Who's Who in Los Angeles,* published in the 1920s, Fremont Place was well represented despite having room for only forty-eight homes (later increased to seventy-three.) A.P.

Giannini, founder of the Bank of America, lived for a time at number 108. Department store heir Adolph Sieroty and his wife Bertha hosted Albert Einstein for dinner at number 85. Across the street from the Mosier-Fifield-Ali mansion stands the most recognized Fremont Place home, famous for its overstated celebrity pedigree. The two-story Beaux Arts mansion was built for Helen Mathewson, former proprietor of the Hershey Arms hotel. In 1918 she rented the home for eight hundred dollars a month to America's leading actress Mary Pickford and her mother. Pickford had recently left her first husband. She lived in the blue upstairs front bedroom at 56 Fremont Place while secretly dating leading man Douglas Fairbanks. They married after several months and moved to their

Mary Pickford spent less than a year living with her mother at 56 Fremont Place, actress Mary Miles Minter not much longer. In their day, the home was visible to boulevard travelers.

A Home on Wilshire Boulevard, Los Angeles, Calif.

Pickfair estate in Beverly Hills. Despite this brief occupancy, Pickford is often mistakenly labeled an early property holder in Fremont Place.

After the Pickfords moved out, actress Mary Miles Minter moved in. The two women had much in common. Both had been teenage stars with blond curls and pixie smiles, and studio executives were grooming Minter to take over from Pickford as America's Sweetheart. Like Pickford, Minter lived with her mother and occupied the upstairs left bedroom. After Fremont Place, however, their life paths diverged, to say the least. Pickford started United Artists studio and reigned as the queen of the film world. Minter enjoyed brief stardom, but her career evaporated in a scandal that still fascinates. In 1922, her presumed lover, Paramount Studios director William Desmond Taylor, was murdered in his apartment near Westlake Park. Both Minter and her mother, reputed to be another of Taylor's lovers, were whispered about as suspects but never charged. Minter's star faded fast. In the 1980s, a television show investigating the case received permission to X-ray the walls of 56 Fremont Place looking for a stashed weapon, but of course nothing was found. The Minters had lived in the mansion for mere months, until Mathewson sold the property in 1920, two years before the homicide occurred. Taylor's murder remains officially unsolved.

Fremont Place, which residents call The Park, remains a favorite enclave for Hollywood celebrities and others who value privacy. Locked gates keep the public off the curving streets with an eclectic collection of architectural styles: brick Tudor, rambling ranch, red-roofed Mediterranean and others. High walls, thorny bougainvillea vines and dense stands of timber bamboo do such a good job of obscuring the view that many Angelenos have never seen Fremont Place. Fewer still probably realize that the mansions were the target of serious overtures to demolish them and build high-rise apartments in the 1960s and '70s.

Sidewalks and ornate Wilshire Special lamps arrived on Park Mile by the late 1920s, but builders were slow to follow. It's the only length of boulevard where lots remain undeveloped, due to deed restrictions and vigilant neighbors. Victory Gardens were planted during World War II.

Those years were a time of transition for all of the neighborhoods along Park Mile. The Watts riots in 1965 and increasing crime rates made the affluent pockets less desirable. Many old-line families left for the suburbs or newer enclaves of wealth such as Bel-Air, Malibu and the Palos Verdes Peninsula. The low point came when an intruder attacked March Fong Eu, the California Secretary of State, in her Fremont Place home in 1986. By the end of the decade, however, Windsor Square and Fremont Place had been discovered again, and property values weathered the real estate recession that followed the 1992 riots. Homes soon began selling for millions of dollars.

The rebound also included Hancock Park, which was the latecomer in the area—developed starting in the early 1920s. Although the entire area of mansions and graceful drives north of Wilshire is often mislabeled Hancock Park, the community encompasses only the streets between Rossmore and Highland avenues. Its initial prestige drew from the opening in 1920 of the adjoining Wilshire Country Club. "Hancock Park was to be the city's most exclusive residential section," early ads by sales agent R.P. Shea promised. In the minds of many, it became just that after Los Angeles annexed the neighborhood in 1923.

Hancock Park, like the other mansion areas, attracted mostly families that were affluent, white and Protestant. The country club set disdained wealth that came by way of Hollywood. Some of that was code for anti-Jewish prejudice, although actors of any background felt the sting of rejection. Wilshire Country Club for many years denied membership to even such big stars as Bing Crosby and Bob Hope. A notable exception was Howard Hughes, who as a youthful millionaire joined country clubs almost as profligately as he made movies and bought airplanes and corporations. Though not an actor, he produced and directed, and eventually owned RKO Studios, and made the gossip columns as a regular at the Cocoanut Grove. While living at his home on Muirfield Road, which overlooked the eighth green, he courted Katharine Hepburn and in some accounts scandalized club members by landing a plane on the fairway with the actress on board.

Dedicated in 1925, Wilshire Boulevard Congregational tried a jazz orchestra to hold off bankruptcy. Rev. Dyer explained, "There is a quality to some church music that depresses modern congregations."

No African Americans could buy in Hancock Park until the late 1940s, when the restrictive covenants in property deeds were ruled unconstitutional. Singer Nat King Cole and his family moved in near Hughes at 401 S. Muirfield and endured a vicious welcome. Neighbors demanded they leave. Someone poisoned the family dog. Cole's daughter, Natalie, remembers an epithet being burned into the front lawn. Such hatred was ironic, since for years bluebloods in Hancock Park and Windsor Square had been commissioning a prominent black architect to design their mansions.

Paul Revere Williams had grown up in Los Angeles and trained at the local atelier of the Beaux Arts Institute of Design. Williams became the first African American to join the American Institute of Architects and later was the first black man honored as a fellow. His career took off in 1920 when he began serving on the city planning commission and working for John C. Austin. He assisted on Austin's design of the Shrine Auditorium, but made his reputation on fine residences. His first important commission, the Leistikow home at 554 Lorraine Boulevard in Windsor Square, came from Austin. Afterward, Williams designed a trio of mansions on Hancock Park's McCadden Place for members of the Banning family. His work in Hancock Park includes an English country estate at 435 Rimpau where, according to local lore, Britain's Prince of Wales (later King Edward VIII) learned how to play craps.

By 1927, Williams was doing so much work along the boulevard that he moved his offices into the Wilshire Arts Building, a popular base for architects at 3839 Wilshire (since razed). He fought past the racism of the day. Potential clients, for instance, often wished to hire Williams based on his reputation, but

"in the moment that they met me and discovered they were dealing with a Negro, I could see many of them freeze," he said in the 1930s. He used a bit of psychology to help them over their discomfort. Williams would invite his flummoxed prospects to reveal their budgets, then reply that he never worked for such a small amount. He followed with a gracious offer to chat informally for a few minutes free of charge. Rather than refuse gratis advice from such a respected architect, many would hear Williams out. Often, he would land the job.

WHILE HANCOCK PARK and Windsor Square set a high bar for affluence, more modest residential districts grew up along the Park Mile. Wilshire Crest advertised in 1920 as "that beautiful subdivision facing Wilshire Boulevard on the high ground just west of Fremont Place . . . Every Wilshire Crest lot is within three blocks of Wilshire Boulevard, not miles away like many so-called 'Wilshire Sections.'" It includes the streets between Mullen and Highland avenues that have come to be called Brookside because of a well-kept secret. Behind some homes on Longwood Avenue, the stream stills flows in *El Arroyo del Jardin de las Flores*.

Impressive homes also used to line Wilshire itself, but they have been lost over time. Two in particular were familiar, tourist-worthy landmarks in their day. Behind a white-picket fence at the northeast corner of Wilshire and Rossmore Avenue stood the home of oil millionaire Jackson Barnett, the so-called richest Indian in America. The elderly Creek, brain

Mullen Park, Wilshire Heights and Ridgewood Park were all middle-class subdivisions alongside the boulevard. Wilshire Crest hyped itself as "the crowning Wilshire development."

damaged since a fall from a horse, came into a fortune after drillers struck oil on his Oklahoma land in 1912. Nine years later he migrated to Los Angeles with his wife Anna Laura Lowe, who was thirty-nine years younger. Usually dressed in a striped suit, he made a daily appearance to direct boulevard traffic in front of

Norma Desmond's ghastly life in *Sunset Blvd.* was fictional, but the mansion she haunted was authentic. Creepy and abandoned, it posed a mystery at 4201 Wilshire for years before Hollywood showed up. The swimming pool where hack screenwriter Joe Gillis floats dead was built as part of the filming fee.

his mansion. Guides steered tourists past the Rossmore corner in the hopes that Barnett would put on a show. After he died, his estate became the focus of a nasty court case that ended with Lowe being stripped of her inheritance and forcibly evicted in front of newsreel cameras.

Another eye-catching mansion sat empty at Wilshire and Irving boulevards for most of two decades. The 1924 relic, the *Times* said, qualified as "a mockery to a man's dream of living in the perfect home." The man was William O. Jenkins, a U.S.

consular agent in Mexico who built the fourteen-room mansion to last, with thick concrete walls and steel crossbeams. He fitted it with numerous custom features, but Jenkins and his family lived there only one year before returning to Mexico. Oil man J. Paul Getty finally bought the empty residence in 1936 as part of a far-reaching plan to control the whole block from Wilshire to Sixth Street, raze every mansion and build the Getty company headquarters. Before he could implement the strategy, though, the home was awarded to his ex-wife in a divorce settlement.

The former Mrs. Getty leased the gloomy residence to Paramount Pictures as the filming location for *Sunset Blvd.*, the 1950 classic starring Gloria Swanson as aging has-been actress Norma Desmond. The swimming pool where hack scriptwriter Joe Gillis (played by William Holden) meets his end was dug for the film. The pool appears again in *Rebel Without a Cause*, the 1955 icon of the street-gang genre starring Natalie Wood, James Dean and Sal Mineo. The Phantom House, as neighbors knew it, remained mostly abandoned until 1957, when it was finally demolished for a six-story office building designed by Claude Beelman and erected by the Getty company where Crenshaw Boulevard dead-ends at the boulevard.

The Getty headquarters was the first glaring intrusion into the Park Mile residential atmosphere. Deed restrictions in 1911 forbade converting most homes into businesses for fifty years, but Getty attorneys won an exemption by arguing that the clause was obsolete—Wilshire Boulevard had become too built up to be reserved for residences. Other owners had to wait until the property covenants began to expire in 1961. When they did, developers rushed in with big plans for apartments and office towers. Intense fights over zoning and future growth led to a 1979 city ordinance creating the Park Mile district along Wilshire and blocking most new commercial use.

Existing businesses could stay. The most noteworthy, other than Perino's, was the home office of Farmers Insurance Group at Wilshire and Rimpau. The elegant building was designed in 1937 with three stories, later raised to seven. Though clearly commercial, its crisp, somewhat Art Deco appearance complements Park Mile's architectural appeal and fits in with the strip's more culturally significant landmarks. Also, since it sits on the south side of the boulevard, its shadow does not fall on any Hancock Park homes.

Park Mile's most visually striking landmark is the Italian-inspired

After a court battle, oilman J. Paul Getty razed the *Sunset Blvd.* mansion in order to build his company headquarters. He tried to buy the entire block of homes between Wilshire and Sixth Street but was rebuffed. One of those homes is now the official mayor's residence for Los Angeles.

church at Wilshire and Plymouth Avenue. Its 144-foot-high tower soars skyward from a bend in the boulevard, so that drivers approaching from the east can glimpse the Historic-Cultural Monument from miles away. It opened in 1925 as a Congregational church, with a pastor, Frank Dyer, who flouted tradition. Some members got upset when he called church music boring and invited a jazz dance orchestra to perform in the new sanctuary. To stave off bankruptcy, he organized a benefit prizefight starring heavyweight boxing champion Jack Dempsey. Ministers across the city deplored the spectacle of church-sanc-

tioned boxing and censured Dyer. Defiant, he hung a banner on the Wilshire façade pleading for donations and sermonized from the pulpit: "Would Los Angeles be safer, saner and finer if all the churches were closed?" In the end Dyer lost the church, which was sold and re-christened Wilshire United Methodist. It was there that seventeen-year-old film star Shirley Temple married actor John Agar.

Its solid-looking neighbor to the west could easily be mistaken for another religious edifice. In fact, the Spanish Colonial Revival structure is the clubhouse of the Ebell of Los Angeles, at one time the

More than one hundred gasoline stations once serviced Wilshire. Fewer than seven remain, none of them in Park Mile. Farmers Insurance Group moved into its three-story building in 1937 and later expanded upward and outward.

country's largest women's club with close to five thousand members. Listed on the National Register of Historic Places, the Ebell has been the scene of innumerable luncheons, weddings, lectures and society cotillions. The club was founded downtown in 1894 at a gathering convened by Harriet Russell Strong, a walnut farmer and the first woman admitted to the chamber of commerce. She was a multifaceted entrepreneur who invented irrigation technology and bred pampas grass as a fashion accessory for women. Strong was hit by a car and died before the Wilshire clubhouse opened.

Designed by Sumner Hunt, the block-long complex contained numerous meeting rooms and halls, plus the attached Wilshire Ebell Theater. Cork floors dampened the sound of clacking heels and impassioned voices at the weekly Monday afternoon teas. Thinking of everything, a member even designed dining room chairs to accommodate hanging purses.

"There is nothing flamboyant about it, nothing bizarre," an architectural journal wrote of the Ebell clubhouse in 1928. The Windsor Square Theater opened at the far end a year earlier, billed as the first stage on the boulevard and just seventeen minutes by bus from downtown. It became the Wilshire Ebell Theater.

Members were the wives of civic leaders, and the Ebell's influence was so great that the governor and mayor attended the club's mortgage-burning party. Ebell ladies formed the city's first Red Cross unit, opened a rest home and famously clashed in 1935 over their taste in art. After artist Maxine Albro painted large frescoes depicting Greek and Roman sibyls, some members complained the female figures were too uninhibited. Journalist Carey McWilliams made light of the hubbub in *Westways* magazine, reporting that the mythical oracles "smirked from the walls and eyed the dowagers with sportive mien." After a split vote, a coat of lye ended the controversy.

Directly across the boulevard, the Wilshire International Pavilion exudes a more modern style. Built in 1961, the clean lines are broken by statues of

The Post-War House showed GIs returning from World War II what they should aspire to in a new Southern California suburban home. Real estate innovator Fritz B. Burns and his friend Welton Becket spent $175,000 equipping the model with "storage wall" closets, double-pane windows, soundproof doors, large-screen television—even washable walls for the kiddies. Visitors crowded in seven days a week until 9 P.M.

Egyptian pharaohs, Roman emperors and George Washington, among other historical figures. The pavilion was designed as a Masonic Scottish Rite Temple by Millard Sheets, an architect and muralist who directed the Otis Art Institute. It was one of his last significant works, and the temple opened to mostly rave reviews—though not from its Hancock Park neighbors. Pushed by the residents, the city restricted use to Masonic events and nonprofit activities such as police funerals and community gatherings. Starved of income, the temple closed in the 1990s. More than a decade later, a developer restored the building, changed the name and reopened with a Masonic heritage museum on the second floor. A seventeen-hundred-seat auditorium, however, still sits mostly unused.

No hidden Park Mile locale collected as much notoriety as the ranch-style model home obscured by a low fence on the southeast corner of Wilshire and Highland Avenue. No one lived there, but thousands probably wished they could. The Post-War House was architect Welton Becket's most unusual Wilshire commission. At the conclusion of World War II, innovative subdivision builder Fritz B. Burns retained Becket to design a model that would display all the modern conveniences available to new suburbanites. Burns sold tickets for a dollar and introduced a million visitors to advances such as electric garbage disposals, two-way intercoms and automatic climate controls. Bathrooms came with built-in sun lamps and tank-less toilets. In the backyard, Becket installed a built-in barbecue with sink and refrigerator area, in a patio area visible from every key room. It was innovative design for the 1940s that became routine in countless Southern California homes. *House Beautiful* magazine devoted a whopping forty-two pages to the Post-War House in its May 1946 issue.

When the crowds dropped off, Burns remodeled and reopened it in 1951 as the House of Tomorrow, with more labor-saving devices and a rooftop heliport. Eventually interest died out and Burns used the model home as his real estate offices.

The Miracle Mile

THE POST-WAR HOUSE
WILSHIRE BLVD. AT HIGHLAND

Hancock Park
...LA BREA TAR PITS

"Movie" Actors

Beverly Wilshire Hotel

Santa Monica

CHAPTER SIX

MIRACLE MILE

NO ONE IN LOS ANGELES pays much attention to statues, especially of real estate men. The life-size bust of A.W. Ross that peers from an island of flowers at the corner of Wilshire and Curson Avenue, in the whiff zone of oily ponds at the La Brea Tar Pits, draws few glances. While Ross was living, friends arranged to have the likeness bronzed and mounted there, adding a plaque that reads:

> *Founder and developer of the Miracle Mile.*
> *Vision to see, wisdom to know, courage to do.*

After a middling half-career, the Miracle Mile was the big score for Ross. He didn't get fabulously rich, though he did all right, but Ross could claim credit for transforming a stretch of empty fields

Innovative architecture helped attract curious visitors—and downtown stores—to the Miracle Mile. Beyond the Art Deco Wilshire Tower, where Desmond's moved in 1929, is the rounded Coulter's department store. It later became The Broadway.

no one wanted into the most famous shopping mile in Southern California. The Miracle Mile in its heyday had the May Company, The Broadway, Coulter's, Desmond's, Silverwoods, Mullen and Bluett, Myer Siegel—old-line downtown stores that bought into the Wilshire Boulevard phenomenon at the right time. The Miracle Mile wasn't for the swells who required the white-gloved attentiveness of Bullock's Wilshire or I. Magnin. It belonged to the masses who packed into clearance sales, grabbed a sandwich at Melody Lane and took coffee breaks under the blue windmill at Van de Kamp's. On the morning in 1948 that Ohrbach's, a New York discount department store,

threw open its doors on Wilshire, so many excited shoppers shoved their way in that radio stations alerted latecomers to stay away.

The Miracle Mile had live Santas and reindeer at Christmas, Easter parades and, in the fall, the University of Southern California homecoming procession. Everyone knew where along Wilshire the Miracle Mile began and ended, at La Brea Boulevard on the east and Fairfax Avenue on the west, with a little slop over at both ends. That's not so true anymore. Since the department stores folded or moved to modern shopping malls, the Miracle Mile has become less identifiable. But it's still an attraction, drawing people to the Los Angeles County Museum of Art, built on the former site of the Hancock family's *Rancho La Brea* adobe, and the George C. Page Museum, repository of the treasures extracted from the tar pits. The

Big crowds watched Sunday air races at the Wilshire and Fairfax airports. Pilot Emory Rogers acquired both fields from their celebrity owners before dying in a 1921 crash. Looking east, the boulevard bends at the tree-shaded La Brea Tar Pits. Oil derricks are off to the left.

Petersen Automotive Museum, the Craft and Folk Art Museum and the city landmark El Rey Theater are located on the Miracle Mile, along with fine examples of Welton Becket and Stiles Clements design and the Googie-style Johnie's coffee shop.

Wilshire Boulevard functions there as the main street of a thriving urban village, the first leg of the grand concourse to exude such a neighborhood feel. Apartments with character from the 1920s and 30s, some of them with city Historic-Cultural Monument status, fill the side avenues. Thousands of people come to work on the Miracle Mile each day. This stretch of Wilshire is the home of magazines, trade newspapers, ad agencies and cable TV networks, with modern skyscrapers mixed in among the landmarks erected in Ross's day.

Ross would approve. From the 1920s into the 1960s, he staked his future on luring Los Angeles to his creation. That he succeeded so well probably stunned his early rivals, who thought Ross ill-advised to pay unheard-of prices for fields of wheat and beans out beyond the city limits. Plenty of factors argued against it working. First were the old *Rancho La Brea* tar pits, interesting to look at, but not a desirable neighbor. They emit noxious odors and occasional burps of flammable gas, and the gelatinous subterranean tar, or asphaltum, has proven impossible to contain. When it wishes, it blurts up through

G. Allan Hancock donated the world-famous tar pits and his family adobe for a county park. Spanish explorers had seen bones stuck in the bubbling ponds, but only in 1906 did scientific digs begin. Saber-toothed cats, wolves and elephants are among the five hundred thousand Ice Age fossils recovered, and one set of human remains. La Brea Woman, as she was dubbed, lived nine thousand years ago.

lawns, sidewalks and cracks in the Wilshire Boulevard pavement. Also, within earshot of Ross's land a forest of ugly derricks slurped crude from the Salt Lake oil field, located north of Wilshire between La Brea and Fairfax. If prospects could ignore all that, there were a pair of noisy, unpaved airfields kicking up dust clouds at Wilshire and Fairfax. Hollywood producer Cecil B. DeMille owned the field on the northwest corner; Charlie Chaplin's brother Syd for a time ran the landing strip on the southwest corner.

Skeptics called the whole idea Ross's Folly. Money men knew Ross as a transplanted Iowan who had shown no superior acumen in his earlier real estate gambits. "Regular investors wouldn't even let me tell my story," he told an interviewer later. "Even friends who had the means to help me laughed and wished me luck." Ross went for it anyway. His confidence came from a simple calculation and a leap of faith. In 1921, the year the Ambassador Hotel opened, Ross pondered the automobile-propelled migration occurring west of Los Angeles. He figured anyone choosing to live in the new outlying areas like Beverly Hills or Hancock Park would prefer to shop close to

Tenants in the new Art Deco office towers could see the Pacific or gaze east and watch Los Angeles spread outward along Wilshire Boulevard. The earliest buildings on A.W. Ross's Miracle Mile, foreground, embraced Spanish styles.

home and avoid the congestion and lack of parking space downtown. Pegging four miles as the magic distance that a shopper would happily travel, he took out his map and drew circles four miles in diameter around the new residential districts. Where the circles intersected on Wilshire Boulevard, he bought up land.

Ross had gambled that Los Angeles would continue to sprawl—always "a sensible hunch," in the words of historical author W.W. Robinson. Ross sold lots first on the south side of Wilshire. The earliest establishments were small storefronts, often with a mezzanine or upstairs studio. Ross called his development Wilshire Boulevard Center until an investor, impressed by the activity so far from downtown, suggested the Miracle Mile sobriquet. "The miracle lay neither in its physical character nor in the complexions of its few, small retail outlets, but rather that it existed at all," historian Richard Longstreth wrote.

In the late 1920s, sensational Art Deco buildings proclaimed to Los Angeles that the Miracle Mile had arrived to stay. Wilshire Tower, between Dunsmuir and Burnside avenues, was designed by Gilbert Stanley Underwood, architect

Arches and simulated cut stone on the Morgan, Walls and Clements-designed Ralphs at Hauser Avenue suggested a Spanish palace. A popular Pig'n Whistle café on the second floor later mounted its slogan on the roof: "Up and Down the Coast." The city landmark market built in 1928 lasted sixty years.

for the spectacularly rustic Ahwahnee Hotel in Yosemite National Park and the United States courthouse downtown. Completed shortly before Bullock's Wilshire, Wilshire Tower surprised drivers on the boulevard with an eight-story Zigzag Moderne shaft of offices that vaulted skyward from a wide Streamline Moderne base—a striking and optimistic structure to find in the middle of bean fields and oil derricks. The Los Angeles Conservancy credits it with helping to set the architectural standard for all of Wilshire Boulevard.

A.F. Gilmore established the boulevard's first gas dispenser in 1909 by mounting a tank on his wagon and parking at the northeast corner of Wilshire and La Brea Avenue. Business was good so he built a station.

Ground-level display windows were trimmed in rich black-and-red granite. The lobby featured fourteen-karat-gold ceiling details. Upstairs offices were small, but you could watch the sun set over the Pacific. Doctors and dentists snapped up space at the prestigious new address, not minding that it was more than five miles out from downtown.

Patients would come because the tower ruled the skyline. It also made the perfect easel to hang a sign on. Desmond's got there first, in March 1929. The original downtown men's hat shop had been in business since 1862. A Desmond's branch in the east wing of the Wilshire Tower building, with a prominent neon sign on the top, gave the Miracle Mile a boost of credibility. Six months later Silverwoods, a

downtown clothing merchant dating from 1892, opened its first boulevard store in the west wing. Desmond's and Silverwoods were not alone among the bean fields for long. Myer Siegel, a downtown women's store known for carrying the latest Paris fashions, opened in 1931 two blocks east on the lower floors of a Stiles Clements Zigzag Moderne tower, the Dominguez–Wilshire Building. A third Zigzag Moderne tower, the tallest yet, went up in a prime location at the intersection of Wilshire and La Brea, which would eventually replace Wilshire and Western as the busiest traffic corner in the city. Meyer and Holler, the firm that built Hollywood's Egyptian and Chinese theaters, designed it for E. Clem Wilson, an Ohioan who made a fortune in the oil-tooling business

Flashing signs were discouraged on the Miracle Mile, but gasoline pumps under airplane wings were fine. First the plane's fabric skin had to be sheathed in metal—fire department's orders. The Flying Saucer, next to Brown's Bakery, had nothing to do with spaceships. Its neon logo was a china plate with wings.

Even banks had artistic verve. A year after Stiles Clements unveiled his renowned 1928 Zigzag Moderne Richfield Building downtown, he copied elements of its black-and-gold design in a branch at 5209 Wilshire. The restored former bank has been nominated for the National Register of Historic Places.

and owned a Fremont Place mansion. The eleven-story tower's most dramatic feature was a dirigible mast poking skyward from the roof, visible for miles and later, high-visibility signs advertising Mutual of Omaha, Asahi beer and Samsung electronics.

Together, the trio of Miracle Mile towers,

plus Wilshire Center's aqua green Pellissier Building and elegant Wilshire Professional Building, comprised the beginnings of a compelling Automobile Age skyline. Impossible not to notice, the enthusiastic structures were "visible from all directions across the basin and hills, and consciously designed as visual landmarks for the sprawling distances of the car city," said architect Alan Hess.

Buildings that attracted attention, that lured drivers to alter their ways, were crucial to Ross's strategy. So when Ralphs wanted to open a supermarket at Wilshire and Hauser Avenue, the company hired Stiles Clements to design a Spanish Churrigueresque eye-stopper, with embellished arches and Baroque flourishes and, upstairs, a Pig'n

Whistle café. It borrowed details from Clements's Chapman Market three miles east, which opened the same year. If Ross had his way, the most dramatic sight on Wilshire would have been a massive forty-story hotel and railroad terminal he proposed to develop in 1929. At the time, City Hall was the only Los Angeles structure allowed to rise higher than thirteen floors. Ross's monolith could be built only because the site, near Fairfax, fell just outside the city's control. The idea, however, perished like so many giddy real estate dreams—crushed by the October 1929 stock market crash that announced the start of the Great Depression.

Had Ross gone ahead, it could have been his revenge on Los Angeles. For four years, he had been

LA-68—"Miracle Mile," Wilshire Boulevard, Los Angeles, California

PHOTO BY "DICK" WHITTINGTON   OB-H2587

The 1931 Dominguez–Wilshire Building kept its distance from Wilshire Tower to preserve the view. Clothier Myer Siegel started downtown at First and Spring streets in 1886 and introduced Paris couture designers to Los Angeles women.

frustrated by politics. Originally, buyers of his Miracle Mile lots had been free to build retail stores because they were beyond the city limits, in unincorporated county territory. In 1925, however, Los Angeles annexed the Miracle Mile and zoned it for residential use only. That satisfied powerful interests downtown and in the Wilshire Center area that feared Ross's Folly turning into competition. Ross appealed to the voters, who had recently opted in favor of commercial development in Wilshire Center, but they rejected his stores and offices amid the oil derricks. Ross lost at the state supreme court too. Ultimately, the Miracle Mile flourished only after Ross learned to cleverly exploit a loophole in the law that allowed for spot zoning—going before the planning commission and city

council on a case-by-case basis to seek individual waivers of the commercial ban. It was painstaking and expensive, but there was a side benefit.

Spot zoning gave Ross extraordinary influence over what got built—much more than was typical for a real estate agent. His buyers would ask Ross for advice on what kinds of projects were likely to win approval. He nudged them toward architectural styles that he thought elevated the Miracle Mile, such as Art Deco, and away from garish displays he found distasteful, such as flashing neon signs. Office towers were kept at least a block apart, which avoided visual clutter and traffic congestion. Ross did apparently enjoy a bit of whimsy. Bob's Airmail Service pumped gasoline and changed tires under the wings of a Fokker

In 1961 the Miracle Mile was a mishmash of architectural styles. Lee Tower at 5455 Wilshire, originally light blue, was the first Los Angeles skyscraper built after height restrictions were eased. Beyond it is the Clem Wilson Building at La Brea.

transport that had flown fifty thousand passengers for Western Air Express before being retired in 1934 to the northwest corner of Wilshire and Cochran. A photography supply store, the Darkroom, opened in 1938 with a storefront that resembled a nine-foot-tall Argus camera made of black Vitrolite. Newsreels flickered in the lens for the pleasure of passers-by. The Flying Saucer Café's neon sign depicted a winged plate.

NOT EVERYTHING IN the Miracle Mile area centered on Ross. Closer to Fairfax, the south side of Wilshire belonged to a competing developer, former silent film actress Ruth Roland. She had made a killing on a lot at Wilshire and Ardmore and invested the profits in a sixty-one-acre wheat field just east of Fairfax. "I am a profound believer in hunches," Roland explained. She guessed right about the future fortunes of Wilshire Boulevard. When her Roland Tract subdivision opened for home sales in 1923 and took off, Roland left her film career behind and became known as a savvy real estate player.

Just west of Fairfax, on the former site of the Chaplin airfield, an unusual planned community tried to compete directly with Ross. Carthay Center sprang from the creative impulse of real estate entrepreneur J. Harvey McCarthy, who hoped to develop an attrac-

Clements's Late Moderne design at 5570 Wilshire featured dozens of garden patches for growing flowers and a mural of the original downtown Mullen and Bluett. The elegant Miracle Mile store opened in 1949 with menswear on the ground floor, women's clothes upstairs.

Prudential Tower, now Museum Square, swallowed up Santa Bonita Avenue and brought the crisp International Style to postwar Wilshire.

tive shopping complex and hotel surrounded by an enclosed neighborhood of Spanish Colonial Revival and Mediterranean-style homes. McCarthy stressed aesthetics in order to set his project apart from all the other developments sprouting around Los Angeles. He had designers master-plan the 136 acres with pleasing, curved residential streets oriented toward a central shopping plaza. Access off Wilshire was via McCarthy Vista, a wide landscaped avenue that helped further distinguish Carthay Center (a deliberate play on the developer's name). The most unique feature was a California history theme. McCarthy's father had been a forty-niner, and the developer himself belonged to the Native Sons of the Golden West, which popularized a romantic version of the state's lore. He named the streets for early California figures such as Commodore John Sloat, the naval commander who captured Monterey in 1846, and José Antonio Carrillo, a colorful Los Angeles *alcalde*. Walkways named for California's Spanish missions connected the streets. Replicas of mission bells lined McCarthy Vista and a granite monument placed at the Wilshire entrance honored Jedediah Smith, the first American to reach California by land. A statue by sculptor Henry Lion commemorating the forty-

niners—a gold panner placed next to a stream with flowing water—stood where McCarthy Vista crossed Eulalia Boulevard (now San Vicente Boulevard).

McCarthy carried the theme into construction of Amanda Chapel, named for his mother. Workers used water from each California mission and sand from all fifty-eight counties to lay the cornerstone in 1923. The chapel (now the Episcopal Church of Our Saviour), Carthay Center Elementary School

LACMA's 1965 dedication created a museum and arts district that pushed the Miracle Mile further from its original focus on shopping. But A.W. Ross approved.

across the street and ads promising that a subway would someday make for a fourteen-minute commute downtown enticed home buyers. But McCarthy never could lure any major stores or a hotel. Merchants preferred the Miracle Mile, which was easier to reach and had open space for parking lots. Instead, McCarthy erected his most successful monument—a stroke of

Carthay Center's 1920s elementary school and chapel, top, survive beside Olympic Boulevard. The hulking Carthay Circle Theatre, scene of glamorous movie premieres, was the main attraction—"a theater masked as a cathedral." McCarthy Vista, the divided avenue in the foreground, leads to Wilshire. At right, Walt and Lillian Disney attend the 1941 debut of *Fantasia* with conductor Leopold Stokowski.

shrewd thinking that made Carthay Center famous.

The Carthay Circle Theater, whitewashed concrete trimmed in blue, with a high bell tower and a neon sign that could be seen for miles, opened in 1926. "Simple, massive and dignified, the building stands out for its intrinsic beauty," *The Architect and Engineer* raved. A theater "masked as a cathedral," *Pacific Coast Architect* wrote. The auditorium was round, with a drop curtain that featured an homage to the pioneer Donner Party, which as every California child learns perished crossing the Sierras in winter. Bronze busts of Native American leaders and photographs of Lili Langtry and other nineteenth-century actors adorned the lobby and lounges.

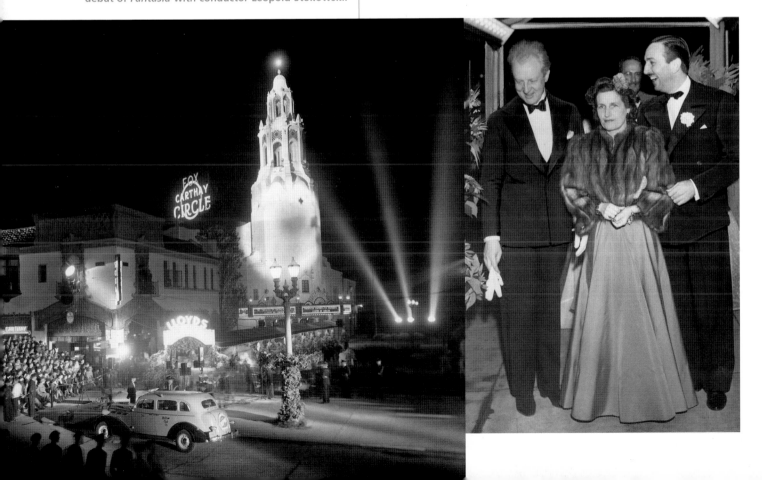

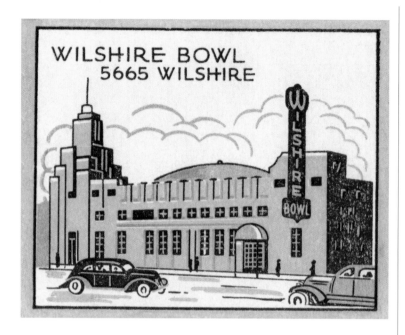

Paintings of historic scenes forty feet tall graced the walls. No movie palace (or subdivision) invested so much in artwork. McCarthy explained his motivation simply: "What Los Angeles needs is more art."

The Carthay Circle, which eventually gave its name to the entire neighborhood, became the showcase Westside movie venue, despite almost closing during the Depression. Premieres at the Carthay Circle evolved into major Hollywood sensations, with lines of Cords and Packards turning off Wilshire and cruising down McCarthy Vista under weaving spotlights. Newspapers reported that thirty thousand fans gathered outside to watch stars arrive for the 1937 premiere of Disney's animated *Snow White and the Seven Dwarfs,* followed two years later by the West Coast debut of MGM's *Gone With the Wind.* For

Two sentimental favorites of Miracle Mile Art Deco fans were torn down to make way for less-exciting buildings. Melody Lane, a Pig'n Whistle spin-off at 5351 Wilshire, dished up fountain concoctions like the Chocolate Shower, the Honey-Do and the Lover's Lane (ice cream soda with mint).

Disney's *Fantasia* in 1940, the most elaborate theater audio system in use at the time, Fantasound, was installed. At the tract's Wilshire entrance, Musso's restaurant—run by a founder of the Hollywood landmark Musso and Frank—grew into a popular boulevard attraction. Opened in 1934 in a model home designed by architects Curlett and Beelman, Musso's served under the stars and advertised as the "most unique and original restaurant in the West."

The Carthay Circle's crowds helped turn the Miracle Mile into an entertainment district. The rollicking Wilshire Bowl on the south side between Hauser and Masselin avenues was a popular nightclub for seeing stars and dancing to well-known band leaders. After World War II it changed to Slapsy Maxie's, the nickname of professional boxer-turned-actor Maxie Rosenbloom. Dean Martin and Jerry Lewis were discovered performing their comedy act at Maxie's and received contracts from Hal Wallis at Paramount Studios for *My Friend Irma*, the first of several Martin and Lewis films. Slapsie's is long gone (it was remodeled as Van de Kamp's, itself now gone), but the 1936 El Rey Theater nearby remains admired for its Zigzag and Streamline Moderne styling. Two other attractive movie theaters faced onto Wilshire just east of La Brea. The Four Star-United Artists, remembered for Art Deco friezes signifying unity and artistry above the marquee, belongs to a church that covered the friezes. The Moorish-style Ritz, at Wilshire and La Brea, was demolished and the site paved for a bank and parking lot.

The Miracle Mile's success, as elsewhere on

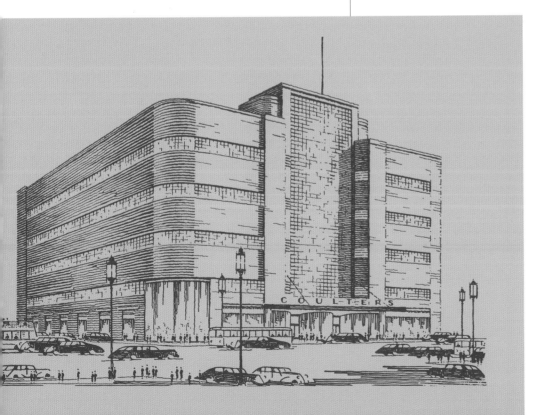

Coulter Dry Goods Co. had been downtown since 1878 so its move to Wilshire made a statement. Coulter's flagship was an exemplar of Streamline Moderne design by Stiles Clements. The Broadway took over in the early 1960s. After the store was razed, pools of oil and tar gathered for two decades in an empty pit at Wilshire and Hauser.

Wilshire, also offered a showcase for architects. Stiles Clements designed the Moderne flagship store for Coulter Dry Goods, which opened in 1938. It stood four stories high, with a streamlined exterior of white concrete rounded at the corners and horizontal bands of glass-block windows. A dramatic seventy-two-foot-high glass-block panel soared above the boulevard entrance. Besides making an architectural statement, the arrival of Coulter's represented a significant milestone for the Miracle Mile. This was no mere branch store, like Desmond's or

Silverwoods. After sixty years, Coulter's left downtown entirely for Wilshire Boulevard.

One month later, May Company announced its own plans to build a lavish Miracle Mile store, at the northeast corner of Wilshire and Fairfax. That had been the site of Sportsmen's Auditorium, a tented exposition grounds for circuses, auto expos and the Los Angeles National Horse Show. May Company engaged the architecture firm of Albert C. Martin, which designed a store that came to be appreciated as one of the most elegant Streamline Moderne structures ever built in the city. A "fitting finale to Los Angeles's Deco decades," UCLA's Thomas S. Hines wrote in the 1994 book *Grand American Avenue: 1850–1920.* The smooth limestone exterior exhibited

The May family bought land at Wilshire and Vermont in 1924, calculating correctly that their department store needed to grow beyond downtown. But they got cold feet and sold the acreage. When the May Company finally got to Wilshire in 1939, it arrived in style.

the rounded Streamline sweep of Moderne but with an electrifying flourish. Decorating the corner above Wilshire and Fairfax was a four-story-high, gold-leaf-and-black-granite design reminiscent of a 1930s perfume bottle. On either side of the bottle, vertical neon letters spelled out MAY CO. The store, which opened in 1939 to instant raves, embraced the latest in Automobile Age practicality: in the rear was the largest parking lot of any store on Wilshire—with space for seven hundred fifty cars—and the first department store service station.

Behind the new May Company along Sixth Street, the Goodyear Blimp would swoop down and pick up paying customers for fifteen-minute rides over Hollywood. Also on Sixth, an innovative housing development began going up on the former oil field. Developed by Metropolitan Life Insurance Co., Parklabrea (its name then one word, usually rendered in formal script) was a bridge between the periods before and after World War II. Planned in 1941 to encompass 2,750 low-rise apartment units, fewer than half were finished before the wartime call on available lumber and steel halted construction. After the war, the concept was rescaled dramatically upward. Eighteen height-limit towers quickly added three thousand apartments to the thirteen hundred already built. Park La Brea, the new spelling, became the West's biggest apartment complex, its residents all instant Miracle Mile shoppers.

The postwar years also ushered in a new era, culturally and architecturally. Business offices inhabited by men in white shirts, ties and felt hats elbowed in among the Art Deco-era stores. Corporate-sponsored International Style buildings appeared, just as exciting but in a different way than the playful examples from the 1920s and '30s. A rectangular edifice just east of the tar pits was designed in 1948 by Welton Becket's firm as the western home office of Prudential Insurance. A fragment of the Rock of Gibraltar, the company's

Wilshire at La Brea was becoming the city's busiest intersection, but May Company's grand opening elevated Fairfax to the Miracle Mile's most fashionable corner. All was well until suburbia and giant shopping malls took away the customers.

symbol, was incorporated into a support column in the lobby. Prudential Tower, the first Wilshire example of the International Style, was promoted as the tallest office building on the boulevard, although its dominant sense is horizontal.

A windowless center shaft, rising 185 feet, is flanked by a pair of ten-story wings. Windows run the length of the open-design office wings, creating alternating bands of glass and white-exterior finish. When illuminated from the inside at night, Prudential Tower appeared to be a negative image of its daylight profile—the windows become the bright bands and the façade shaded. The effect was no accident, and neither were the slender palms planted to cast vertical shadows on the Wilshire face of the center shaft. The Prudential Tower "gives focus to the erratic skyline of the entire city," *Arts & Architecture* enthused. "A sentinel by day and a beacon by night, it has become to the millions of people who live within its compass a symbol of their city and the western way of life."

Becket moved his offices into the tower, and Ohrbach's took three lower floors. Ohrbach's profitable modus operandi was to purchase Paris couture fashions from prominent designers like Dior and Givenchy and within eight days have inexpensive copies on the racks. At the southeast corner of Wilshire and Fairfax, Becket's firm designed another postwar Miracle Mile landmark—this one short-lived. The Japanese-themed Seibu department store became an exotic shopping destination, known especially for its rooftop garden, koi ponds and Japanese restaurant. The store stayed in business for just three years after opening in 1962, then was replaced by a relocated Ohrbach's.

The Miracle Mile's reputation as a shopping wonderland faded with the arrival of more office buildings. After the city relaxed its ban on skyscrapers in 1957, the twenty-two-story Lee Tower went up on the site where Bob's Air Mail had dispensed gas under an airplane wing. An unremarkable black-glass box to contemporary eyes, the building was light blue when it opened in 1961, with a rooftop helicopter port. At Wilshire and Hauser, California Federal Savings and Loan erected a twenty-eight-story home for itself. Chairman J. Howard Edgerton had opened his first savings and loan on the same block in the 1930s, and the diamond-shaped, Charles Luckman-designed tower became, in the words of *Westways* magazine, the "prestige location of the prestige section of the city's prestige street." It too had a heliport with room for six aircraft.

The tallest spire on the Miracle Mile is the white, thirty-two-story People's Bank building at 5900 Wilshire Boulevard. Constructed in the early 1970s for Mutual Benefit Life Assurance, the office tower occupies a block that has been the focus of numerous aspirations. In the mid-1930s, architects Paul R. Williams and Richard Neutra designed model homes that were built on the site for the California House and Garden Exhibit. In 1938, plans were announced for a forty-two-hundred-seat, French Renaissance-style opera house and twelve-story office tower, but the project fell through. Grocery store magnate Huntington Hartford attempted in the 1950s to build a complex with a twelve-hundred-seat legitimate theater, office building and television-and-radio production studios. He ended up opening a theater in Hollywood instead. In 1964, a developer proposed a complex called Wilshire Square that was to comprise two facing towers of luxury apartments, twenty-two and twenty-eight stories high, with retail stores at the base. It also never happened.

While those projects faltered, the most important presence on the Miracle Mile took over the park acreage directly across the street, on the site of the former Hancock family home. A.W. Ross predicted that the Los Angeles County Museum of Art, the largest new art museum in a quarter century when it opened in April 1965, would bring a million visitors a year to his Miracle Mile. He wasn't far off. LACMA has become one of the city's most visited art repositories. The collections cover all eras in the history of art, and special exhibits regularly attract long lines.

Three original buildings designed by William L. Pereira Associates faced onto Wilshire from a raised plaza, with fountains and a reflecting pool along the boulevard. The waterworks were filled in a decade later, in part out of concerns about oil and gas seepage, and replaced with a sculpture garden. In the mid-1980s, a major renovation radically altered the face that the museum presents to Wilshire Boulevard. The Robert O. Anderson wing, housing

Simon's ran lunch counters downtown, but in 1935 its owners asked architect Wayne McAllister to design an eye-grabbing chain of drive-ins. His sleek Moderne circle at the northwest corner of Wilshire and Fairfax made for stylish chili and burgers.

the twentieth-century art collection, placed an imposing wall of glazed limestone and glass block right up against the sidewalk. Visitors enter off Wilshire through a narrow, shaded passageway, almost the antithesis of the dramatic invitation made by the broad front steps of the Metropolitan Museum on Fifth Avenue in New York. Almost ever since, there have been discussions about surgically altering the presentation with a grand new design.

A.W. ROSS DIED in 1967 as a success, with a home in Beverly Hills and membership in the exclusive Los Angeles Country Club. He did not live to see the Miracle Mile lose its major stores to shopping malls and changing tastes. The Clements-designed Ralphs

market and a later Citizens National Bank branch were torn down. The architect's store for Coulter Dry Goods also was razed, after two decades as The Broadway. "This used to be quite a shopping center," a distressed clerk poured out to the *Times* during the store's final week in 1980. "All the old L.A. families shopped around here. It doesn't look like a miracle anymore." The May Company closed in 1993 when the chain merged with J.W. Robinson's, but not without some growling from loyalists. The pink fifth-floor tearoom had its own community of habitues who gathered daily to eat lunch and play cards. Routines were so ingrained that when an estranged husband came in and shot his seventy-nine-year-old wife and then killed himself, some patrons pleaded with police officers to be allowed to finish their game of panguingue.

Simon's gave way in 1955 to Romeo's Times Square, which got a new Googie dining room and a simple slogan that would have worked for the coffee shops that followed: "Wilshire at Fairfax. Always Open." Menu graphics show how the aesthetics of the corner evolved with time.

The May Company building was saved by LACMA, which made it part of the museum. Another significant save occurred in 1986 when the Petersen Automotive Museum salvaged the former Ohrbach's and Seibu store at Fairfax. Named for Robert E. Petersen, a magazine and book publisher, the museum's location on a prominent corner on the boulevard of the Automobile Age could not be more appropriate. The Petersen's three hundred thousand square feet are dedicated to the history of the automobile and its role in the evolution of Los Angeles and its culture. The original four-story Becket design was partially remodeled by architect Marc Whipple of the Russell Group—the new façade on Wilshire resembles the fins that decorated the rear of many 1960s automobiles.

The corner of Wilshire and Fairfax has also been the home of a succession of eateries for at least seven decades. After the Simon's drive-in closed, the design team of Louis Armet and Eldon Davis built the New York-themed pizza and coffee shop Romeo's Times Square. It opened in 1955 with faux New York scenes and garish lighting in keeping with its prominent corner location and open-all-night policy. By 1960 Ram's had taken over, but it soon morphed into Johnie's, which has been praised as one of the best remaining Googie-style coffee shops designed by Armet and Davis. Even before closing in 2000, Johnie's was a popular filming location. Much of the 1988 cult favorite *Miracle Mile* takes place at Johnie's. In the later, less-serious film *Volcano*, Wilshire Boulevard itself is consumed by a river of molten lava that erupts from the tar pits.

CHAPTER SEVEN

BEVERLY HILLS

MIDWAY BETWEEN DOWNTOWN and the beach, Wilshire Boulevard slips free of the municipal clutches of Los Angeles and enters another world, planet Beverly Hills. The Fifth Avenue of the West crowd of the 1920s and 30's would approve. For a bit more than two miles through the enclave made famous by movie stars, campy television shows and ostentatious displays of wealth, Wilshire Boulevard became what the boosters always envisioned: a prestige business address, home to coveted stores and hotels, and a reputation for affluence so accepted that no one blinks when an acre of vacant dirt sells for almost ten million dollars.

In Beverly Hills, street numbers and the snob factor divide into classes at Wilshire. Everything costs more to the north, uptown in what author David Weddle calls "America's Palatine Hill, the

Mary Pickford and her filmland pals woke up sleepy Beverly Hills with an assist from refined hotels and memorable architecture along Wilshire.

sacred high ground where its demigods—movie stars, industrialists, Wall Street wizards, rock icons, media and fashion moguls—took up residence in some of the most lavish, phantasmagoric mansions the world has ever seen." The flats to the south are less exclusive, derided as Baja Beverly Hills. An address on the boulevard itself—that commands more respect than anywhere else along Wilshire's flow to the ocean.

The boulevard's last serious shopping district is there: Saks Fifth Avenue, Tiffany and Co., Neiman Marcus, Barney's New York, among other stores. For a historic landmark of national prominence, there's the Regent Beverly Wilshire, where the emperor of Japan, Prince Charles of Great Britain, first ladies and Elvis Presley have slept. In architecture, there are I.M. Pei's sleek headquarters for the Hollywood powerhouse Creative Artists Agency and movie house designer S. Charles Lee's "Spanish Art Deco" Wilshire Theater. The boulevard's elite stature is achieved without a single skyscraper. The city's tallest structure tops out at fourteen stories—the Beverly Wilshire's Beverly wing, where actor Warren Beatty occupied a penthouse for a full decade.

Beverly Hills did not yet exist in 1895 when Gaylord Wilshire cleared his boulevard beside Westlake Park. The first streets were not platted until 1907. On the original maps, the route destined to become Wilshire was merely the southern edge of town. Oil man Burton Green and partners had begun in 1900 to drill on the former Mexican rancho called *Rodeo de las Aguas,* "the gathering of the waters." The name refers to the runoff streams from Benedict, Franklin and Cold Water canyons that splashed across the arid rancho. Green's wells never located much oil, but they tapped enough of another valuable under-

ground resource—water—to suggest he rethink his business. With plenty of water, real estate was the way to go. The newly formed Rodeo Land and Water Co. set out to establish a town where others had failed.

The first attempt to establish a town on the future site of Beverly Hills was made by German-born pharmacist Edward A. Preuss in 1869. He paid $10,775 for 3,608 acres of the former *Rodeo de las Aguas,* which had belonged in California's Mexican era to Maria Rita Valdez de Villa, a soldier's widow of African and Hispanic heritage who supported eleven children. She defended her title to the rancho against raiders, conniving relatives and nefarious Americans, but finally was forced by financial troubles to sell for four thousand dollars in 1854 to Henry Hancock (future owner of *Rancho La Brea,* to the east) and Benito Wilson, owner of *Rancho San Jose de Buenos Ayres,* west of Doña Valdez's land. The pair wanted to grow wheat, but after Hancock sold his share the rancho was dedicated to sheep grazing. When Preuss took over, he cut up the land into five-acre parcels and called his ill-timed, German-inspired farming settlement Santa Maria. Los Angeles Avenue through the center of town, such as it was, approximated the later route of Wilshire Boulevard. A smattering of farms were sold, but Santa Maria did not survive a searing drought in the 1870s that left rotting livestock carcasses on the pasture lands that surrounded Los Angeles.

Next came Los Angeles hoteliers Henry Hammel and Charles Denker. They bought the acreage and grew crops for the kitchen of their prominent United States Hotel. During the late 1880s boom that lured Gaylord Wilshire south from San Francisco, some Los Angeles investors figured the area just west of the Hammel and Denker property would be ideal for a settlement called Morocco. It would fall midway to the coast on the Los Angeles and Pacific Railroad, which acquired a right-of-way across the ranch and laid tracks. Morocco, located about where Wilshire and Santa Monica boulevards would later intersect, proved to be too remote to make much speculative sense. The railway, though, looked like a decent bet. It provided another easy

Ranching still had a future on the coastal plain west of Los Angeles at the time Gaylord Wilshire invented his boulevard—or so people thought. Until it was sold to developers, the Hammel and Denker dairy supplied the hoteliers' downtown kitchens.

route to the beach and connected all the way to the inland San Fernando Valley via the Ostrich Farm Railway to Burbank. For one summer in 1889, the venture flourished. By October, however, heavy rains washed out the tracks and there was no money to replace them. Morocco soon vanished.

More than a decade later, it was Burton Green's turn. His company acquired 3,055 acres of the old Valdez rancho; the $1,222,000 investment was probably the best buy any of the partners ever made, seeding several fortunes. With such a large swatch of

Horticulturist John J. Reeves was commissioned to decorate the barren streets of Beverly Hills with exotic pines, laurels, eucalyptus and of course palm trees. To enhance the town's beauty, he devoted a single species to each main avenue.

acreage in one company's control, Beverly Hills became one of the first Southern California towns to be comprehensively planned and built with a "satisfying neatness of execution," British architect Reyner Banham wrote. The concept came from New York landscape architect Wilbur Cook, who had worked with Frederick Law Olmsted Sr. on the White House grounds. After reaching Los Angeles in 1905, Cook helped with plans for Exposition Park, portions of Griffith Park and the downtown Civic Center. Later, he contributed to the design of Carthay Center.

Cook's master plan for Beverly Hills urged that the town grow along the railroad line from Los Angeles, a well-traveled route that became Santa Monica Boulevard. He created gently curving resi-

dential drives with names like Canon, Rodeo and Crescent that glided north toward the hills. Large homes and estates would be at the upper end, in the canyons. Lesser but nice homes would be built below the main road that became Sunset Boulevard. Stores and the homes for service workers were confined to the wedge formed by the tracks and Wilshire Boulevard, which crossed at the west edge of town. Green named his settlement after reading about President William Howard Taft vacationing at Beverly Farms in Massachusetts. "Beverly Hills is indeed a paradise of beauty, culture and art . . . overlooks the Wilshire Boulevard district and occupies a position which may be said to command Hollywood," ads by sales agent Percy H. Clark proclaimed in 1907.

For all the careful planning, the venture faltered. To juice up sales, Rodeo Land and Water picked a picturesque hillside to build a scenic hotel that would spur curiosity about the town. The Beverly Hills Hotel, a visual delight with Spanish-style arches, palm trees and rambling gardens, became a popular stopover between Los Angeles and the coast. It succeeded in igniting interest. Even so, when early citizens proposed to incorporate as a city, they could only obtain the five hundred required signatures by coaxing itinerant laborers to pose as residents. The city's status became official on January 2, 1914, but it took six more years before a fortuitous event made Beverly Hills a familiar name. As Banham put it: "The success of the whole project probably depended more than anything on the Fairbanks/Pickford household deciding to move there."

Mary Pickford was the biggest movie star Hollywood had ever produced, and she was one of the country's most powerful women. Douglas Fairbanks, ten years older, was the debonair leading man of social comedies who would, after their marriage, star as a swashbuckler in adventures like *The Three Musketeers, Robin Hood* and *The Thief of Baghdad.* Having recently co-founded United Artists studio with Charlie Chaplin and D.W. Griffith, Pickford and Fairbanks were an intriguing cultural force, the biggest celebrity power couple. Before their marriage in March 1920, Fairbanks had acquired an old hunting lodge in Benedict Canyon. Using designs from architect Wallace Neff, the couple redid the lodge as a twenty-two-room mansion and called it Pickfair.

The fourteen-acre estate on Summit Drive featured wandering streams, a white sand beach and an Olympian swimming pool. It became one of the world's most celebrated homes, praised by some as America's Buckingham Palace. Britain's future King George was among the royals who supped at Pickfair's legendary garden parties and formal dinner soirees, where the guests might also include Albert Einstein arraying the silver and china to explain his breakthrough theory of relativity. At a meeting in the Pickfair living room, plans were hatched for creation of the Academy of Motion Picture Arts and Sciences, the Oscar-awarding institution that is still located on Wilshire Boulevard in Beverly Hills. Fairbanks served as the first president.

With Mary and Doug in charge, Beverly Hills became the star colony that more restrictive communities such as Hancock Park and Windsor Square never could. Chaplin, Rudolph Valentino, Buster Keaton, Gloria Swanson and Harold Lloyd moved in. (Lloyd's lavish estate, Greenacres, is listed on the

Beverly Hills had two swimming pools for every Bible, Rogers famously said. His newspaper columns spread the movie star colony's name.

National Register of Historic Places.) Cocoanut Grove habitues such as Norma Talmadge and Marion Davies drifted west to buy or build substantial homes. Thomas Ince led the migration of studio heads, followed by Louis B. Mayer, Samuel Goldwyn and Carl Laemmle. Packard dealer-to-the-stars and neon-sign pioneer Earle C. Anthony never made the move personally, but his Greene and Greene house on Wilshire Boulevard did. Actor Norman Kerry purchased it in 1923 and moved the home to 910 N. Bedford Drive, where it remains.

Presiding gently over that early Beverly Hills society was Will Rogers, the most admired American wit of the time. As honorary mayor by acclamation until his death in a 1935 airplane crash, Rogers did his part to promote the colony. He put a Beverly Hills dateline at the top of his nationally syndicated newspaper columns and sang its praises in speeches. He never forgot, however, who made Beverly Hills. His most important function, Rogers quipped famously, was to direct lost tourists "to Mary's house."

WHEN THE STARS began settling in, Wilshire Boulevard through Beverly Hills was just a narrow strip of oiled macadam, barely wide enough for a comfortable motoring lane in each direction. Plowed fields lay on both sides of the road, and a scenic row of mature eucalyptus trees stretched for a full mile from Preuss Road (later renamed Robertson Boulevard) to Wilshire's junction with Santa Monica Boulevard. The trees were probably planted as windbreaks, but the foliage also served to shield the view of a popular attraction that for four years, beginning in 1920, probably lured more visitors to the city than even Mary Pickford.

The Los Angeles Speedway, beside the south frontage of Wilshire Boulevard, satisfied Southern Californians' craving for the rabidly popular sport of automobile racing. In February the national racing circuit would begin its season at Beverly Hills, move east to places like Indianapolis and Daytona, then return at Thanksgiving to crown the year's champion driver. Crowds of fifty thousand and more packed the covered grandstand off Pico Boulevard or parked in the weeds along Wilshire, then climbed into the cheaper, sun-facing bleachers. Cars raced on a 1.1-mile oval-shaped track with a wood surface—two-by-four planks laid on edge and steeply banked so racers could take faster turns. Fast being relative—the opening day race in 1920 was won with an average speed of 103.2 miles an hour.

Investors, including Louis B. Mayer, saw the speedway as a way to tap the wallets of passionate racing fans. Until then, races had been held on Wilshire Boulevard and other public streets in the city of Santa Monica. Huge crowds poured into Santa Monica to watch the road races for free, but moving the competitions onto a track meant that fans could be tagged eight to ten dollars for box seats, five dollars for reserved seating in the grandstand and two dollars for general admission. In 1924, more than eighty-five thousand attended the final Beverly Hills race. The winner, a young driver named Harlan Fengler, closed the era by setting a new world record with an average speed of 116 miles an hour. By then the speedway had outlived its time, much like the

Gently curved avenues lent the fledgling town a pleasing design sense. But it took the shocking pink Beverly Hills Hotel, beneath the hand-drawn arrow in 1920, to light a fire under land sales. Below Wilshire is Los Angeles Speedway.

SANTA MONICA BLVD.

WILSHIRE BLVD.

airfields had at Wilshire and Fairfax. The wood track needed costly repairs, but the bigger factor was that—in the midst of the 1920s population boom—attractive land beside Wilshire Boulevard would bring a substantial price from real estate developers. Beverly Hills was becoming hot property.

Real estate broker Frank Meline, who had exclusive selling rights to many streets, ran ads illustrated with palm-lined avenues converging on the lush Beverly Hills Hotel. The pitch: "Why invest in a home site in an inferior location when we are offering such values in Beverly Hills today . . . right in the heart of the frostless belt." The less desirable, undeveloped south side of Wilshire, where the track had been, became the province of another seasoned land seller, Walter G. McCarty. His ads asked potential buyers to visualize the empty corner of Wilshire and Beverly Drive turning into the future heart of Beverly Hills and his Beverly Vista subdivision into the "finest residential district in America." In case prospects scuffing their shoes in the dirt failed to see what McCarty saw, he entertained them with free airplane rides and the chance to win a Chandler touring car.

Steep turns and a wooden banked track encouraged speedway drivers to go faster than they could in road races. The *Times* estimated that 93,000 spectators watched the 1923 "Turkey Day" championship—and that several fainted after seeing two men killed in a pre-race accident.

McCarty was not above a bit of deceptive showmanship to sell lots. Architect S. Charles Lee's first job in Los Angeles in 1921 involved duping the suckers at a McCarty tract closer to downtown. Lee revealed later that a favorite McCarty tactic was to block Sunday traffic by parking a tractor in the middle of Wilshire Boulevard. As unwary motorists waited and fumed, a salesman would pick out a likely prospect, jump on the running board and offer to steer them through a shortcut out of the traffic jam. The route invariably wound past several lots for sale, with the agent pitching the whole time. His hard-to-refuse offers would include a private meeting with the "architect"—Lee, installed by McCarty at a drafting table back in the sales office, collecting a hundred dollars apiece for house plans.

McCarty was in Beverly Hills for the long haul, much as A.W. Ross was on the Miracle Mile. Both were developing at the same time, just a couple of miles apart. McCarty's kept his offices at Wilshire and Speedway Drive (later renamed El Camino Drive) and borrowed a tactic from Burton Green's Rodeo Land and Water. He too built a hotel of fulsome beauty and eye-pleasing proportion, the most plush lodging

Thanksgiving Day racing began at 1:30 P.M. "as a concession to the gentlemen who eat their turkey early in the day, and will be over by 4:30 . . . out of regard to those who want to eat afterwards."

on Wilshire west of the Ambassador Hotel. McCarty's Beverly-Wilshire apartment-hotel opened New Year's Eve in 1927 on an entire block of the boulevard, with extensive gardens behind the main building. Designed by Walker and Eisen—who in addition to the Gaylord on Wilshire were the architects of the highly regarded Fine Arts and Oviatt buildings in downtown Los Angeles—the Beaux Arts-style hotel stood nine stories tall and packed in three hundred fifty rooms. Gracious chandeliered dining rooms and ballrooms and a marble lobby—entered from the boulevard under a dramatic arch—helped lure an elegant trade. A "Parisian orchestra" entertained at luncheons, with a fashion review every Wednesday. Since the city of Los Angeles forbade Sunday dancing, that became the big night for a hop out Wilshire Boulevard to swing in the hotel's Gold Room.

As Wilshire Boulevard grew up, Beverly Hills evolved from an exclusive show business colony into

California Bank's Art Deco wedding-cake tower still beautifies the boulevard, but the Warner Bros. Beverly at 9404 Wilshire has been demolished. The photograph looks west, the postcard east past the long-vanished Brown Derby and the mosque-like Beverly Theatre.

more of a real town. The population exploded from seven hundred in 1920 to seventeen thousand a decade later, but the sensibility remained exclusive and mannered. Home buyers were required to landscape and forbidden to cut down street trees—the "eighteen

thousand uniformly planted pines, acacias, blue-flowering jacarandas, feather pepper or scarlet-flowing eucalyptus trees that line the thoroughfares," as a guidebook put it. FOR SALE signs, a staple of the boom era, could be only one foot square. Residents fought moves by Los Angeles to swallow puny Beverly Hills through annexation—unlike Venice and other cities that gave up their independence, Beverly Hills pumped enough water to resist the expanding empire.

At the opening on May 18, 1925, the Beverly Theater and vaudeville playhouse showed a filmed tour of nearby stars' homes. Many of the Moorish flourishes have been stripped off, but close examination of 206 N. Beverly Drive will reveal some original details.

Upstart Beverly Hills even began, literally, to outshine Los Angeles. At a civic ceremony in September 1927, actress Corinne Griffith flipped the switch on 243 new Wilshire street lamps. That was five months before the mass illumination of Wilshire Specials on the Los Angeles end of the boulevard. Griffith was another example of an actress who, like Ruth Roland along the Miracle Mile, invested wisely and made a stunningly profitable transition to the land game. Her investment acumen, or her good luck, became legendary when it was discovered years later that she owned all four corners at Beverly Drive and Charleville Boulevard, one block removed from the commercial epicenter of Wilshire. Even Pickford dabbled in real estate. At the southeast corner of Wilshire and La Cienega, she jumped into the 1930s miniature golf craze and opened the jazzy French Deco-styled Wilshire Links. The course was designed for Pickford by a United Artists art director and built by studio workers.

As occurred elsewhere on Wilshire, the Beverly Hills stretch became decorated with appealing Art Deco specimens. It was the Roaring Twenties, and developers had permission to be daring and modern. The California Bank tower at 9441 Wilshire, across from the Beverly Wilshire Hotel, fit the bill. It was designed to stack like a wedding cake by architects John and Donald Parkinson and opened the same year as their Bullock's Wilshire masterpiece. Beverly Hills also sought to compete with the opulent movie theaters opening farther east, such as the

One superb 1920s drive-in market survives on the boulevard, and it wasn't typical. The Clock Market at 8423 Wilshire, which became a Porsche dealership, had a seven-room apartment upstairs. Note the Sunset gas pumps and signs for fruits and vegetables.

Carthay Circle and the Wiltern. The city's first cinema, erected as the Beverly in 1925, still stands at Wilshire and Beverly Drive. The Moorish-style domed theater has been gutted and occupied, at times, by the flashy Fiorucci boutique and an Israeli bank, but it still contrasts nicely with the newer, plainer buildings on the block.

S. Charles Lee's Fox Beverly Hills movie palace, one mile east along Wilshire, opened in 1930 across Hamilton Drive from the Pickford links. *Southwest Builder and Contractor* called the twenty-five-hundred-seat, black-and-silver architectural piece the "ultimate in dazzling and daring." Fox regarded it as the studio's flagship movie house outside of downtown, and a vice president even lived in the apartment at the top of the tower, under a tall neon Fox sign. The auditorium survives, without the sign, as a live performance venue called the Wilshire Theater. Not so the Warner Bros. Beverly Theater, built four blocks east of the Beverly Wilshire Hotel. The design by B. Marcus Priteca was praised as "late-1920s Art Deco with a Mexican flourish," with a vertical sign spelling out the Warner name in neon lights. Neighbors, however, grew tired of competing with the theater for parking and in the late 1980s opposed preservation moves. It was razed to make way for a bank branch.

Also at Hamilton Drive, across from the Wilshire Theater, a car dealership occupies a 1920s survivor that is even rarer than movie palaces. The drive-in Clock Market was an early version of the ubiquitous contemporary mini-mall. Built in an arc bent around the open parking lot, the Clock had bays inside for a half-dozen grocers and other purveyors. It resembled a dozen Wilshire Boulevard drive-ins, but stood apart from the other markets thanks to an unusual flourish. Over the main building rose a tower—suggestive of Art Deco—that contained a residential apartment.

BEVERLY HILLS' TRANSITION from a movie star outpost sped up when fine department stores and restaurants began filling in open blocks along Wilshire Boulevard. W&J Sloane, the leading downtown Los Angeles furniture store, opened a Beverly Hills store in 1935, designed by the Parkinsons at 9536 Wilshire Boulevard. Two years later, the prominent New York retailer Saks Fifth Avenue chose Beverly Hills for its first Southern California location, at 9600 Wilshire Boulevard. Saks teamed the Parkinsons, who did the exterior, with Paul Williams, who polished the look and styled the interior like a fine residence. Carpets ensured a dignified serenity. Display areas were enclosed almost like rooms, so customers would not be distracted by other shoppers. Williams experimented with lighting regimes to create the desired sense of soft, luxuriant surroundings, even coating the ceilings with a silk-and-rayon finish to dull any glare. Shopping at Saks became an enduring Wilshire Boulevard tradition (and for a time, Perino's even operated a café on the roof).

Next door at 9634 Wilshire, Myron Hunt's I. Magnin in 1938 embraced the future potential of Beverly Hills. Unlike his marble palace for the Magnin family in Wilshire Center, which opened a year earlier, the Beverly Hills store adopted the carpeted hush of Saks. Beverly Hills lacked a shopping palace with the stature of the Parkinsons' Bullock's Wilshire, but in other ways it was catching up to Wilshire Center and the Miracle Mile. A Brown Derby opened across from the Beverly Wilshire Hotel at Rodeo Drive. On Beverly Drive, the venerable Victor Hugo—"unexcelled in the art of serving fine food"—escaped from downtown to reopen closer to where its fine-dining customers now lived.

Romanoff's, at 326 N. Rodeo, became the most popular Beverly Hills star dining room of its day (with the possible exception of Chasen's). Studio moguls Jack Warner and Daryl F. Zanuck and actor Cary Grant were partners, but it was Michael Romanoff's ego-stroking charm and outlandish profile that made it work. He spoke with an Oxford accent and claimed to be Russian royalty, but was unmasked as a Lithuanian Jew born Hershel Geguzin who spent part of World War I in an English jail as a "rogue of uncertain origin." His dogs Socrates and Confucius ate at his table, with plates of their own, but his Hollywood friends didn't care. They put him

in their movies, and he gave them the best tables and a respectable place to hang out. Booth one belonged to Humphrey Bogart, whose regular lunch began with Scotch and soda, followed by an omelet, French toast, milk and coffee, then brandy to finish.

The scene continued when Romanoff's moved in 1951 to a larger location below Wilshire, at 140 S. Rodeo. It was there, shortly after William Randolph Hearst died at the nearby home of Marion Davies, that her new husband got into a fistfight with Hearst's oldest son. Such publicized Hollywood occasions just brought Romanoff's more attention. When Jayne Mansfield's breasts upstaged Sophia Loren in a legendary photo, and feuding gossip columnists Hedda Hopper and Louella Parsons famously made peace, the restaurant benefitted. Eventually, the proprietor's conservative politics and friendship with FBI Director J. Edgar Hoover gradually estranged him from many stars, and the restaurant's trade slowed considerably after Bogart died in 1957. Romanoff's finally closed on New Year's Eve in 1962.

Increasingly, Wilshire Boulevard's skip through Beverly Hills has been turned over to serious commerce. Office and bank buildings of medium height and mixed

Life magazine called phony prince Michael Romanoff "the most wonderful liar in the twentieth century." He had to borrow plates from Bob Cobb's Brown Derby next door to open his Rodeo Drive hangout. They chatted at a 1939 Red Cross benefit at Hollywood's Clover Club.

distinction, most of 1960s and '70s vintage, line the sidewalks. On the corner at La Cienega, where Mary Pickford had her mini-golf links, the first elliptical-shaped office building in the western United States—designed by William L. Pereira Associates —was built in 1972 for Great Western Savings. A statue of actor John Wayne, the institution's long-time television spokesman, stands on the building's east side. At Wilshire and McCarty Drive, the arched and stark white Perpetual Savings building resembles the Wilshire Colonnade complex five miles to the east— both were executed by architect Edward Durrell Stone. The Manufacturers Bank building at Wilshire and Roxbury Drive was described by architecture critics Gebhard and Winter as a "curtain of black glass that undulates around the corner." But the queen of the boulevard remains the Beverly Wilshire Hotel, listed on the National Register of Historic Places since 1987, despite having been extensively altered on the inside.

Walter McCarty's hotel was bought in 1945 by Arnold Kirkeby, a millionaire investor who positioned the hotel as more of a resort. He dressed up the faded jewel with a membership pool and spa, the

Carpenter's near the northwest corner of Wilshire and La Cienega's Restaurant Row offered car service and pure frozen orange juice for ten cents. From 1946 to 1981 it was the Dolores drive-in.

Copa Club, and added tennis courts. Exhibition matches starring champions such as Pancho Gonzales and Bobby Riggs were featured until the courts were converted to parking in the 1950s. Kirkeby sold in 1958 to New York hotelier Evelyn Sharp, and in 1961 the property was taken over by Hernando Courtright, the dashing former general manager of the Beverly Hills Hotel. Courtright, half-Irish and part-Basque (his real name was Bill), affected a Hispanic visage, riding in local parades as a vaquero. He redid the hotel's woody, traditional Oak Room into the more playful Hernando's Hideaway, with Mexican dishes. Of more consequence, Courtright guaranteed discretion for stars.

An out-of-state visitor in 1938 marveled in the *Times* that the Wilshire Coffee Pot looked like its name and the Brown Derby really did have a hat. The home of Ben Hur coffee and melted cheese on toast was in the 8600 block.

He steered the Beverly Wilshire's image toward an elite preserve for celebrities and traveling royalty. He spent lavishly on favors and promotions and wrote letters to heads of state encouraging them to visit. In one resplendent flurry, the hotel hosted Emperor Hirohito of Japan (who desired peeled grapes), the king of Tonga (thirty Big Macs), King Olav of Norway, Denmark's Queen Margrethe and First Lady Betty Ford. On arrival, prominent international visitors would see the flags of their home countries flying on Wilshire Boulevard. At departure the staff lined up for a formal sendoff. Courtright added the fourteen-story new wing, delayed when Welton Becket died during design in 1969. Italian stonecutters were brought in to install a cobblestone driveway between the two sections of the hotel, illuminated with lamps from Edinburgh Castle in Scotland.

Courtright grandiosely called it El Camino Real, the name of the old Spanish King's Highway through California. In 1985, Regent International, a Hong Kong luxury hotel chain, bought out Courtright and gutted the original hotel, modernizing and enlarging the rooms. The official name became the Regent Beverly Wilshire, with 395 guest rooms and suites.

Its competition since 1955 has been the mid-century modern Beverly Hilton, designed by Becket, just west of the junction with Santa Monica Boulevard. Originally the flagship hotel of the world-wide chain run by Conrad Hilton, it has changed hands several times and undergone renovations. The ballrooms and rooftop L'Escoffier dining room became frequent haunts for Hollywood events, and when President John F. Kennedy was in town, the Hilton served as his western White House. Lyndon B. Johnson also stayed there while president. Together, Beverly Hills' hotels, stores and offices form the most assertively affluent commercial stretch found on Wilshire Boulevard. That status appears likely to continue, though as in other segments of the boulevard, a change in direction is underway. Developers are taking a gamble and adapting older commercial buildings to residential use, or erecting luxury townhomes from the ground up. For the first time, Wilshire Boulevard in Beverly Hills could become a prime place to live.

After United California Bank opened in 1962, travelers on Wilshire could see the vault in the round annex. Four decades later it became a high-visibility sports club.

The Beverly Hilton and sculptor Merrell Gage's 1931 electrified fountain are visual landmarks where Wilshire crosses Santa Monica Boulevard. Gage taught at the Chouinard Art Institute.

CHAPTER EIGHT

WESTWOOD AND HOLMBY HILLS

LEAVING BEVERLY HILLS the boulevard stops aiming seaward in a flat straight line and assumes a curvier, more vivacious personality. Wilshire arches and dips and shows off some surprise moves, starting with the incline just past the city boundary where drivers often feel the urge to punch the gas pedal and run a little wild. Along this short strand of raceway there are no stores or office buildings, just high fences screened with privacy hedges and prominent signs on every pole warning motorists never to stop.

Hiding from view there is the most private and splendid playground for the rich to be embedded in the urban sprawl. The Los Angeles Country Club's two tree-lined courses are renowned among golfers,

Architects Allison and Allison designed Wilshire Boulevard Temple, Royce Hall on the University of California at Los Angeles campus and the 1929 Janss Investment Co. headquarters on Westwood Boulevard. It was also put in service as a bank, record store and restaurant.

and challenging enough that they could qualify to host prestigious professional tournaments such as the U.S. Open. The membership won't have it, though. It would mean letting spectators tromp the club's magnificently arboreal grounds. Admittance has always been tightly controlled, a guest invitation to play highly prized. Although bias against Jewish and

minority members has faded, there remains a stubborn disdain for anything Hollywood. The club once rejected matinee idol Victor Mature even after he pleaded that his body of work in fifty-six films proved conclusively that he was no actor.

"Eligibility for membership is a Hoover button, a home in Pasadena and proof positive you never have had an actor in the family," Pulitzer Prize-winning sports columnist Jim Murray once wrote in *Golf Digest*. Probably the only Hollywood star wholly acceptable to the club's patricians was Ronald Reagan,

Westwood Village, Holmby Hills and UCLA were built on the rolling hills above Wilshire Boulevard under a master strategy for developing the last rancho west of Los Angeles. The new campus straddled the ravine to the left of the rectangle of trees.

and when he dropped in for lunch Secret Service agents tagged along. Given the high capitalist tone, it's at least a little ironic that a charter member was social-ist gadfly Gaylord Wilshire. The creator of Wilshire Boulevard joined with banker Joseph Sartori and other businessmen to start what began as the Los Angeles Golf Club. It was formed shortly after two brothers visiting from England, Walter and Harry Grindley, laid out tin cans on a sandy Santa Monica polo field in 1897 (located on the future Wilshire Boulevard) and played Southern California's first holes of golf.

The club established the city's first golf course on Pico Boulevard near downtown. In 1911 the club moved to three hundred twenty rolling acres of ranchland straddling the unpaved western extension of Wilshire Boulevard. Members walked packed-earth fairways and sank putts on oiled-sand "skins." To get there they rode the train to the crossing of Wilshire and Santa Monica, then waved a lantern or sema-phore toward the clubhouse. If they were spotted, a driver came down to pick up the arrivals. Motorists who traveled the dirt boulevard beyond Beverly Hills learned to watch for men in knickers and caps—the third hole crossed Wilshire until 1921 (underground tunnels later connected the north and south courses).

After bisecting the club, Wilshire Boulevard sashays around a bend and into another affluent envi-ronment so unexpected that one wonders: is this the never-realized Fifth Avenue of the West? Marching to the west from Comstock Avenue are two rows of res-idential towers, some of the most precious boulevard

Where the town of Sunset failed at the corner of Wilshire and Beverly Glen, passersby interested in buying a piece of Westwood land could climb the observation tower and get the big picture.

frontage ever sold in Los Angeles. Condominium units on upper floors with views of the country club and the city—plus doormen, valet service and private elevators—fetch millions. A half-acre wedge of vacant land used as a Halloween pumpkin patch and Christmas tree lot at Comstock sold in 2003 for a reported twenty-one million dollars. For that starburst price the developer acquired the official city blessing to erect a condo tower twenty-one stories high, overlooking the secretive fairways.

The golf course, condos and winding avenues lined with mansions that ramble north of Wilshire belong to the community of Holmby Hills. Residents there have included Frank Sinatra, Bing Crosby, Humphrey Bogart and many later stars, plus the architect Welton Becket. Along Wilshire Boulevard, the high-rise corridor of apartments and condos is also known informally as the Platinum Mile. It's a colony of high living for Beverly Hills mansion-dwellers looking to downsize, retired celebrities and cash-laden professionals who value privacy and doting service. At the west end, the residences give way to corporate office towers clustered around the hyper-intense intersection of Wilshire and Westwood boulevards, and to Westwood Village, regarded in the 1920s as the best-planned new shopping district in Los Angeles.

Not so long ago, all of this belonged to one savvy investor. Arthur Letts, who founded the Broadway department store and gave his blessing to Bullock's, bought the former *Rancho San José de Buenos Ayres* after World War I, when Wilshire Boulevard closer to Los Angeles was already a preserve of hotels and apartments. Like many of the men who played in the real estate game, Letts considered the 3,296-acre barley and sheep-grazing spread the prize of prizes—the last big intact domain between Los Angeles and its westward destiny. To get it, he persuaded a reluctant family to sell by presenting them with two million dollars in cash.

The rancho's first owner Don Maximo Alanis had been a Spanish soldier and a settler of the Los Angeles pueblo. It changed hands several times before being purchased in 1884 by John Wolfskill, a Kentucky-born forty-niner and former state senator who paid ten dollars an acre. His dream was to watch the rancho bloom into a town. He built a big white house with fine satin wallpaper about where Santa Monica Boulevard now meets Veteran Avenue, and leased plots to barley growers. Their children played in ponds and springs and listened to the old man's outlandish predictions that Los Angeles, then ten miles distant, would someday envelop their barns and swimming holes.

Wolfskill's first nibble came from speculators offering a hundred dollars an acre for enough land to establish a town they called Sunset, on a rise west of the Morocco station on the Los Angeles and Pacific railroad. In exchange for eight hundred town lots, the railroad paid half the cost of laying curbs and water lines and grading streets. The main street, called Sunset Boulevard, roughly followed the future route of Wilshire Boulevard. The Grand Hotel was built near what became the intersection of Wilshire and Beverly Glen boulevards. An edition of the *Sunset Enterprise* told of a "fountain of youth" hidden in the nearby hills and declared the new town blessed with "rich soil, splendid climate and a fine view . . . above the fogs." But like Morocco, Sunset couldn't survive the railroad's failure. The Grand Hotel was used to store hay before burning down, and Wolfskill got his land back.

Wolfskill kept the rancho together after that, figuring it would be worth more someday. He sold off just three hundred acres, to the rich men of the Los Angeles Country Club. After Wolfskill died in 1913, his heirs refused offers to sell (except for some rugged canyon land spun off for the development of Bel-Air Estates) and waited for a cash deal. Letts came along six years later, loaded with cash.

He acquired a huge swath that stretched from the Beverly Hills line west to what would become Sepulveda Boulevard, and from Pico Boulevard on the south up into the hills of the Santa Monica Mountains. Mostly barley fields and pasture, the land was an alluring mix of flats suitable for inexpensive neighborhoods of small bungalows and more valuable view lots. Eager to develop, Letts turned to the Janss Investment Co., the biggest residential sub-divider in Los Angeles. Peter Janss was the family patriarch, while his sons Edward and Harold ran the day-to-day business. Letts knew his new partners well, since his daughter Gladys had married Harold Janss. The company began well south of Wilshire by offering lots for sale in a new district they called Westwood.

The name acknowledged the hopes of Letts and the Jansses. They promoted Westwood as a western version of Hollywood, promising movie studios and quality stores as well as homes. Fox took the bait and bought a big parcel on Pico to establish a major studio, later merged and called 20th Century Fox. Silent film star Harold Lloyd built a small studio at Santa Monica Boulevard and Overland. What distinguished Westwood, however, was affordable neighborhoods. Like a machine, tracts of forty to sixty acres each were improved with streets and sidewalks

Potential buyers lined up in 1935 to get a look inside an "El Ranchito" model home on Warner Avenue in the Westwood Hills tract. The Janss name is stamped on most residential sidewalks in the community of Westwood.

then put on the market, one after another. To avoid monotony in design, no single building contractor could erect more than a smattering of homes in each tract. At the northeast corner of Wilshire and Beverly Glen an enclosed observation tower covered with incandescent lightning bolts invited motorists to stop, climb up and take a glimpse of the big picture—a new community rising on rolling hills with the Pacific beckoning in the distance. If you were shopping for a lot, you tried to spot it from the tower.

Though it never grew into the next Hollywood, fledgling Westwood hit the jackpot by attracting something even better than studios and

department stores. From the start, Letts had talked up his land as the ideal locale for a University of California campus, knowing it would bring prestige. He had entrée to official discussions as a trustee of the State Normal School, a two-year teacher-training campus on Vermont Avenue attended mostly by women. After much lobbying by Los Angeles interests, the Normal School in 1919 became an adjunct of the university in Berkeley. Even though more students enrolled at Berkeley from Los Angeles than from any other area, the faculty and administration fiercely resisted splitting into a second campus. Only after Los Angeles threatened to establish a separate state university system that would compete for dollars, students and prestige did the Berkeley establishment relent. In 1923, the year that Letts died, the Normal School was formally elevated in status and renamed

Wilshire at Westwood Boulevard would later become the boulevard's busiest intersection, but around 1930 it looked wide open approaching from the east. A sign for Hi-Ho Café, Westwood's first drive-in, is barely visible past the buildings at left. The village is to the right.

the University of California Southern Branch, belittled as "the Twig" by cross-town rivals at USC.

When it came time for the university's Board of Regents to choose the site of a permanent campus, the momentum favored Letts's land. A blue-ribbon committee of seventeen Los Angeles businessmen inclined toward Westwood. Henry O'Melveny, the chairman, was still pushing then for his Wilshire parkway and residential promenade, which would have passed through the community. Members included Joseph Sartori of the Los Angeles Country Club and *Times* publisher Harry Chandler, a major real estate player. Good competing offers came in from Burbank, Pasadena, Fullerton and Palos Verdes Estates, among other places—all offering free land—but the university regents in 1925 anointed what it called the Beverly site. The regents cited the west-

ward trend of Los Angeles—meaning the Wilshire Boulevard phenomenon—but allowed that "the splendid topography and climate of the site chosen were also compelling arguments."

Having the University of California at Los Angeles campus as the centerpiece of Westwood was a priceless windfall for the Jansses. Almost immediately, the company's ads touted the future university as the best reason to buy: "Future prices here cannot even be guessed." Even so, Janss Investment refused to donate the necessary land—brushy, treeless rolling hills cut with a shallow ravine, roamed by jackrabbits, feral dogs and rattlers. The firm insisted on selling

Westwood Village was intended to function as a regional shopping district and, crucially, to be seen by motorists passing on Wilshire. An undeveloped strip along the boulevard was maintained as a landscaped buffer until the office buildings began to go up in the 1960s.

three hundred acres at two thousand dollars an acre and another seventy-five acres for seventy-five hundred dollars, money the university itself could not legally spend. To pay the Janss ransom, students and community groups handed out leaflets and produced a ten-minute film extolling the potential benefits. Voters in Los Angeles, Beverly Hills, Santa Monica and Venice approved bonds to pay for the land, on the basis that every city would benefit from the campus. Work began with the ceremonial turning of the first shovel on September 21, 1927, and construction of a Romanesque-arched bridge over the ravine.

By then, Wilshire had been improved out to Westwood and Janss had begun to sell lots north of the boulevard. Holmby Hills, situated on the most picturesque terrain in the tract, was the company's gem. Named for Arthur Letts's English home, Holmby Hills estates were roomy—one to four acres each with bridle paths connecting to the adjacent country club. Homes had to cost a minimum of twenty-five thousand dollars, a mark of prestige, purposely set five thousand dollars more than in nearby Bel-Air Estates. Designs also had to pass critique by a review board. The Janss brothers sent a clear message to Los Angeles society by personally relocating from Windsor Square to Holmby Hills mansions designed by Gordon B. Kaufmann, later the architect for the *Los Angeles Times* building downtown. Holmby Hills received a further imprimatur of social approval when the prestigious Westlake School for Girls moved there in 1927.

Arthur Letts Jr. seconded his father's vision by erecting a thirty-room Tudor mansion on a large piece of land adjoining the country club. A believer in bigger-is-better, he planted a grove of coast redwoods and other lavish landscaping. The house itself had eighteen fireplaces and a great hall finished in Botticini marble. The Letts estate always had plenty of admirers, but its profile jumped to new heights when *Playboy* magazine publisher Hugh Hefner purchased the property in 1971. He installed a pool, grotto and exotic menagerie. Despite its notoriety, the Playboy Mansion is not the most lavish Holmby Hills property. That claim can only be made by the fifty-six-thousand-square-foot French chateau-like manse built in the 1980s by television series creator and producer Aaron Spelling. He demolished the former home of Bing Crosby, at Mapleton Drive and Club Drive, and oversaw construction for years. As the work dragged, the media depicted the home as a symbol of celebrity excess and Spelling became the object of some ridicule—an offended neighbor dismissed the mansion as look-at-me-I'm-rich architecture.

Holmby Hills, though, always welcomed spectacular homes and quirky homeowners. When studio head Walt Disney moved to North Carolwood Drive in 1950, he laid tracks for a small-gauge train that circled his property and called it the Carolwood–Pacific Railroad.

UCLA TURNED INTO a fine consolation prize for Westwood. Campus and community grew up together, though not always in friendly coexistence. The Westwood Hills neighborhood east of the university became so desirable that homes were priced well beyond the means of most professors. The campus itself evolved into a crowded, frenetic mishmash of architectural styles and parking structures that fills every original acre plus more, spinning off noise and traffic into the residential areas.

The scene bears little resemblance to the quiet, hilltop campus with an ocean view that greeted students in 1929. Most were women, since that was who trained to become teachers at the old Normal School. Men did not comprise the majority at UCLA for eight more years. At first, the entire campus consisted of four warm-red brick Romanesque halls facing one another across a muddy quad. The architects hoped the setting would evoke thoughts of a picturesque town in Lombardy. Royce Hall's arresting bell towers, arches and arcade borrow strongly from the Church of St. Ambrosio in Milan. Elements of St. Ambrosio are also echoed in Powell Library. Haines Hall and Kinsey Hall share the Northern Italian ambiance. Under the guidance of architects David Allison and George W. Kelham, the campus grew to ten buildings, all in the European style, by 1932 when Los Angeles hosted its first Olympic Games.

The fledgling university, with its rugged ravine and pretty setting, became a pride and a curiosity in 1930s Los Angeles, another reason to dress up for a scenic weekend drive out Wilshire Boulevard. Orchards of citrus and other fruit trees covered the lower end of campus, adding to the allure. An unusual feature of UCLA is that Sorority Row was located east of the campus while fraternities were built far away on the west side. The separation has been traced to the primness of the first dean of women, Helen Matthewson Laughlin, who prevailed on the Janss company to keep the sexes well apart. As a result, the ravine that plunged through the school grounds became a meeting spot, apparently the scene of many nighttime trysts. Just south of campus, the Janss brothers fulfilled the rest of their real estate vision with a carefully thought-out college town and shopping district.

The Westwood Village concept was largely the work of Harland Bartholomew, the urban planner who with Frederick Olmsted Jr. in 1924 had inspired the transformation of Wilshire into a grand boulevard. His plan embraced a faux-Mediterranean theme, with angled streets and irregular blocks so the small enclave would feel larger and more inviting. Many corners featured handsome tile-roofed Spanish Colonial Revival buildings with walk-through plazas and upstairs studio or office arcades. In style it resembled downtown Santa Barbara, as that coastal city was rebuilt after the destructive earthquake in 1925. Bartholomew's partner L. Deming Tilton had worked on the Santa Barbara design. "It's a real village in the American sense of the word," French

Like so many episodes in Los Angeles history, the development of UCLA was at least partly a scheme to sell real estate. By that measure, it was hugely successful.

writer Simone de Beauvoir concluded after a visit to Westwood. "It has its main street, stores, banks and drugstores, and around this commercial center it has its residential neighborhoods."

The village purposely sat back off of Wilshire, with the boulevard frontage left free of buildings and planted with low shrubbery so motorists could catch glimpses of the stores, movie theaters and gas stations. Towers lit in neon beckoned to Wilshire traffic from several roofs. Palm trees waved in the median of Westwood Boulevard, the wide avenue that curled through the village and across campus. Signs at the Westwood turnoff on Wilshire greeted visitors to "America's most unusual shopping center." Many of the original buildings remain. At Westwood Boulevard and Lindbrook Drive, the Spanish Revival-style corner with fast-food shops and a movie theater—formerly the Bratskeller, a popular date restaurant—is listed on the National Register of Historic Places. The arched, faux masonry design by

Russell Collins was built as a Ralphs market.

David Allison, architect for the first UCLA buildings and numerous Wilshire Boulevard churches, designed the domed edifice at Broxton Avenue, one of the village's most distinctive sights. It was built originally as the Janss company headquarters and later housed a bank and a restaurant. A former Bullock's store designed by the Parkinsons at Westwood and Weyburn faces across the intersection at the Holmby Building, an intriguing structure with an attractive clock tower, designed by Gordon B. Kaufmann. UCLA's first women's dormitory was located upstairs. Around the corner on Le Conte Avenue, today's Geffen Playhouse was designed by Morgan, Walls and Clements in the late 1920s as a clubhouse for students affiliated with the Masons.

Already gone are a Sears Roebuck and Co. store that was on Westwood Boulevard and a row of Spanish Colonial Revival gasoline stations along Lindbrook. Also gone are the amusements that made

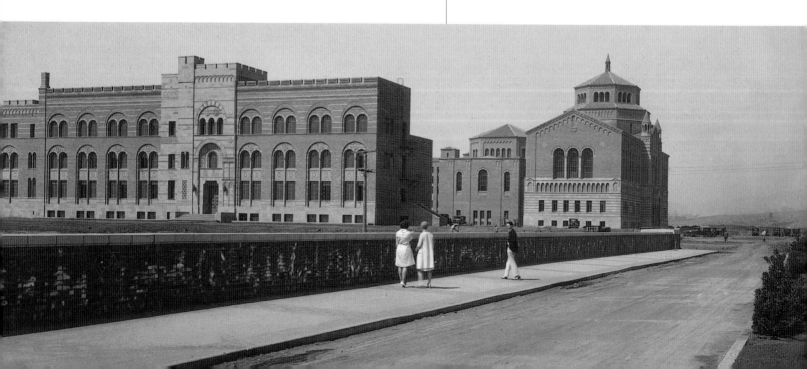

Westwood Village something of a fun zone in the 1930s and '40s—miniature golf links, a bowling alley and an outdoor ice rink. For ten years after it opened in 1938, Tropical Ice Gardens was one of Westwood's most peculiar features. It featured year-round public skating "under California's tropical sun and magic moon," in a mock Alpine village west of Gayley Avenue at Weyburn. Ten thousand spectator seats circled the rink, which became home ice for the All Year Figure Skating Club, an enduring Los Angeles athletic institution, and Saturday night college hockey matches. Tropical Ice Gardens appeared in so many films starring Norwegian Olympic champion Sonja Henie that people referred to it as her rink, though she never actually owned it.

Movie theaters, more than anything, changed Westwood Village from a sleepy shopping colony into a major entertainment district. The landmark Fox Theater at Broxton and Weyburn, opened in 1931, has been called Spanish Colonial Revival in

Italian influences shaped Royce Hall's towers and other original UCLA buildings. After World War II, partners Welton Becket, left, and Walter Wurdeman abandoned the Romanesque style in favor of the jumble of modern architecture that now fills the campus.

style with a touch of Moderne. The Art Deco tower poking over the rooftops sported a neon sign reading FOX, the letters angled, according to legend, so that mogul William J. Fox could glimpse them from his offices at the studio on Pico. Inside, vaulted ceilings and a bas-relief mural lent a sense of celebration and opulence to the lobby. Opposite the Fox is the Bruin Theater, designed with verve in 1937 by S. Charles Lee in keeping with his personal mantra, "The show starts on the sidewalk." An exuberant entrance flows seamlessly into the lobby, and the marquee of flashing neon wraps horizontally around the corner to be viewed from all four directions.

For most of three decades, the Fox and the Bruin were the only two village movie screens (the Crest, formerly the Uclan, opened in 1941 south of Wilshire.) They remain favorite venues for studio premieres, complete with red carpets, paparazzi and gawking fans. Westwood's cinema offerings exploded in the mid-1960s when the Laemmle chain opened art houses, bringing the village a new hip cachet and young crowds. *A Man and a Woman,* directed by Claude LeLouch and starring Anouk Aimee, opened in 1966 and played for ninety-six weeks, according to unofficial Westwood historian Steven Sann. The village became the venue of choice to see event movies like *Love Story,* with Ryan O'Neal and Ali McGraw, which played for an entire year. At the height of New York filmmaker Woody Allen's popularity in the 1970s, his literate comedies screened first in Westwood Village to sold-out houses, the crowds reciting witticisms from previous Allen films as they queued up outside. No lines, however, topped those

Norwegian skater Sonja Henie's films for 20th Century Fox could play at the studio's Spanish Art Deco theater, just behind the Tropical Ice Gardens.

for the fright film *The Exorcist,* which took over the National theater the day after Christmas 1973 for an extended exclusive run. Theater owners took notice of the huge crowds and soon Westwood had seventeen movie screens. Every major Hollywood release waited to debut there.

This was the peak of the postwar baby boom's teenage and college years. Student-age partiers from all over the Los Angeles basin overran the village on weekend nights, along with hippies, cultists and political protesters. Westwood's popularity eventually surpassed the locals' tolerance. Moviegoers took away parking spaces from the stores, but the students didn't buy much. Westwood was so crowded and seemingly successful, no one thought to worry too much about the competition from newer shopping malls and movie theaters. A series of tragic incidents, however, effectively finished off the village as a playground.

On the eve of the 1984 Olympics, with Westwood poised to host prominent events, a disturbed young driver plowed along a sidewalk, killing a teen visitor from New York and injuring more than fifty others. About the same time, youth gangs joined the Westwood scene, adding a violent side to a fairly mellow milieu. Fears of violence exploded into reality on a Saturday night in January 1988, when a gang member from South Los Angeles fired a handgun at a rival on crowded Broxton Avenue. Karen Toshima, a twenty-seven-year-old from Long Beach on a date, was hit. By the time she died twelve hours later, Westwood had been splashed all over the news as the latest turf to be seized by young street thugs. The threat was partly overstated, but also partly true.

Police tried barricades to keep cars out of the village and thin out the crowds, but merchants complained that only kept away paying customers and left behind troublemakers. A couple of window-breaking rampage incidents involving young men led to TV images of police in riot gear. Suddenly, parents stopped

Westwood Boulevard invited visitors into the village. Prominent on the right side are the landmark Ralphs market and Janss headquarters. In the distance is the Fox theater. Art Deco gas stations on Lindbrook Avenue compete for the eyes of Wilshire drivers in the left photograph.

letting their teenagers come to Westwood Village. Customers switched to the newly revived Third Street Promenade in Santa Monica or the mall in Century City, built on the old Fox backlot. Major films stopped opening in Westwood. When Macy's abruptly closed in 1999, the village was without a department store for the first time in almost seven decades.

UCLA students were left as the main patrons, but the village is not well-suited to service as a true college town. It is too quiet at night, since dance clubs are not allowed, and there are not many cheap coffeehouses. Rents are too high to encourage the clothing, music and art stores that appeal to students in funkier districts such as Silver Lake and Venice. The closest general bookstore is a half-mile from campus, across Wilshire in a stretch of Westwood Boulevard called Little Tehran, more a part of Westwood's prosperous Iranian community than the UCLA orbit.

El Paseo at Weyburn and Broxton avenues has been the site of student favorites Tom Crumplar's and Mario's Pizza. The stairs and courtyard, hidden by past renovations, were recently uncovered.

WILSHIRE AT WESTWOOD may be the most imposing of the forty thousand intersections in Los Angeles. Catching a red light ensures a long stoppage while a wave of cross traffic, left-turners and pedestrians takes precedence. Crossing on foot is not for the slow or bashful. Getting across Wilshire requires a high-visibility crosswalk stroll past ten lanes of windshields filled with impatient drivers. No median breaks up the journey—you either make it across on the green light or you suffer the consequences.

The corner is the post-millennium counterpart to 1920s Wilshire and Western—the most intense daily collision of cars, buses, pedestrians and commercial ambition in Los Angeles. The garden-like landscaping buffer between Wilshire and the village succumbed long ago to high-rise development. Tall office buildings enclose both sides of the boulevard, forming a mini-downtown of a dozen towers contained in less than a quarter-mile of Wilshire frontage.

What changed was the opening in 1962 of the San Diego Freeway, a half-mile west of the intersection. It made quiet little Westwood Village

freeway-close to everywhere. Entry and exit ramps at Wilshire force the boulevard into service as a commuter artery to Beverly Hills, Santa Monica, UCLA—the busiest campus in the city—and Westwood's concentration of office towers. Housed in the cluster at Wilshire and Westwood is Occidental Petroleum, the boulevard's largest remaining corporate headquarters, plus technology and entertainment companies, brokerages and an entire tower filled with UCLA administrators.

The first two buildings to alter the village atmosphere went up on the north side of Wilshire, flanking Westwood Boulevard. They met with mostly derision. "The effect is deplorable. Westwood Village by the UCLA campus, with its well laid out winding streets and low buildings, had developed over the years a character of friendliness and intimacy. This has been largely destroyed by the two tall intruders," *Western Architecture* magazine complained. The higher and more attractive building, occupied by

Walkable angled streets gave the village a Mediterranean feel, but in the 1960s high-rise offices, first-run movie theaters and mercury vapor street lights robbed Westwood of its original charm.

Nearly all of the pre-war apartments that used to line the boulevard through Westwood are gone. Chateau Colline at 10335 Wilshire, bottom, is an exception. Dwarfed by high-rise condominiums, the 1935 complex is listed on the National Register of Historic Places.

Occidental and the UCLA Armand Hammer Museum, was designed by Claude Beelman and resembles in some details his headquarters for Getty Oil built five years before on the site of the *Sunset Blvd.* mansion in Park Mile. The Westwood Building was commissioned by Arnold Kirkeby, at the time the millionaire owner of the Beverly Wilshire Hotel. He had taken control of Westwood Village from the Janss company in 1955, and he intended the high-rise, to be called Kirkeby Center, as his personal headquarters. Kirkeby died, however, before it could be completed.

Just to its west, the twelve-story Westwood Medical Plaza is unremarkable except for a quirk in the Paul R. Williams design. All sides are glassed except the west end, which overlooks Los Angeles National Cemetery. Williams apparently felt that the clients of a medical building should not see thou-

sands of grave markers. Instead, the solid west face has come to be used as the tallest and most dramatic advertising space found anywhere on Wilshire Boulevard, visible to travelers on the San Diego Freeway and occasionally controversial due to the political nature of the messages.

Personal tastes vary, but the most architecturally striking among the Westwood office buildings might be the green-and-yellow twenty-four-story tower at 10940 Wilshire. Designed by noted Chicago Postmodern architect Helmut Jahn, its nonrectangular shape creates some excitement on the skyline. Murdock Plaza, designed in 1981 by the architecture firm Langdon and Wilson, stands out as well with a red-brick exterior and such nice touches as a polished granite lobby. Built at the southwest corner of Wilshire and Westwood, Murdock Plaza was commis-

sioned by billionaire investor David Murdock as his home base. The most striking feature is the top-floor Regency Club created by Murdock as an exclusive retreat for business leaders to dine together and entertain clients. Murdock demanded the cuisine meet high standards and employed a number of respected chefs including Joachim Splichal, who would go on to start the successful Patina group of restaurants in Los Angeles. For a time, the Regency's general manager was H. R. Haldeman, the Watergate scandal figure who had been chief of staff to President Richard Nixon, and the club has been the setting for many Republican gatherings and fundraisers. Murdock,

Westwood's skyline of million-dollar condos and Postmodern office towers defines the most aggressively vertical segment of the boulevard. It forms a mini-downtown on the Westside, eleven miles from Wilshire's starting point at Grand Avenue.

though, insisted from the start that the club be open to Democrats, women, minorities and celebrities. Members included football star O.J. Simpson, before his trial and acquittal on murder charges in the 1990s, and actor Arnold Schwarzenegger, long before he became California's governor.

As offices moved in along Wilshire, cultural landmarks from early Westwood necessarily vanished. The first high-rise to leap across to the south side of Wilshire—a Tishman project designed by Charles Luckman in the late 1960s—claimed the site of Truman's drive-in, a burgers-and-malts hangout for a generation of Westside high school and UCLA students. Before Truman's, the southeast corner of Wilshire and Westwood had been the location of the Hi-Ho Café, the first Westwood drive-in popular among students. The luxurious Center West high-rise at Wilshire and Glendon Avenue claimed a Ship's coffee shop that had served patrons twenty-four hours a day for twenty-seven years. Googie-architecture fans regarded Ship's as a particularly fine example of the genre by the design team of Louis Armet and Eldon Davis, and mourned its closure on September 20, 1984.

Neighborhood discontent over the twenty-two-story Center West led to changes in the way high-rise projects are approved in Westwood. Unless the political sense changes, no more office towers will be built on Wilshire. The city imposed zoning and other restrictions near Westwood Village, in part to avoid further congestion. Buildings are subject to approval by a design review board composed of architects and citizens. Beyond the village, however, the corridor of high-rise condominiums and apartments extending into Holmby Hills continues to add new sights to the skyline.

Back when UCLA opened, the most substantial structure on this part of Wilshire was the impressively spired Westwood United Methodist Church at Warner Avenue. The boulevard gradually filled in with garden courts and other low-rise apartments, some of them quite striking, nearly all of them now gone. The best survivor is Chateau Colline, a turreted castle-like fantasy at 10335 Wilshire Boulevard. It was entered on the National Register of Historic Places in 2003 after the owner sought a demolition permit. What spurred the change of residential Wilshire from small, attractive apartment houses to high-rise towers was the city's 1957 relaxing of height limits on new construction.

The first tall building to go up was Wilshire

Ship's earned a loyal following for its toasters on every table, real cream for coffee and the Googie architecture of Armet and Davis. The architects also designed Johnie's on the Miracle Mile.

Terrace, a co-op designed by Victor Gruen Associates and built by Tishman at Wilshire and Beverly Glen's northeast corner, the same spot as the observation tower used to sell Westwood lots in the 1920s. In the 1970s, a real estate boom accelerated the switch to high-rise. Wilshire's older apartments began being converted into condominiums or torn down to make space for new luxury buildings. Prices escalated as the best units with views were grabbed up. One penthouse was put on the market for eleven million dollars, with a Rolls-Royce included. In just a few years, ten new buildings were completed. Then it all lurched to a halt. Money became tight in the early 1980s and the affluent stopped buying, wisely deciding to wait for prices to plunge. Some developers went into foreclosure, leaving projects unfinished. The Blair House, then called the Evian, sat with its steel girders rusting in the Westside fog for eight years. Nearby, the incomplete poured-concrete Park Wilshire also baked in the sun for years. Both uncompleted skeletons served a stark warning to investors to be careful. Both buildings changed hands before being finished at the end of the decade. The penthouse advertised at eleven million dollars sold for under four million dollars.

In the 1990s, however, any doubts about the Platinum Mile as the most desirable high-rise residential district in Los Angeles vanished. Young professionals and stars with money to spend moved in, bringing down the average age and turning up the heat on the market. A seventy-eight-hundred-square-foot penthouse with just three bedrooms on the top floor of a twenty-six-story tower listed for fifteen million dollars.

The building pace slowed after the city designated Wilshire through the high-rise district as a scenic corridor. Limits cap the height of most new construction at six stories. Exceptions are allowed for previously approved projects, provided they won't intrude on the sunlight of nearby homes for more than two hours a day. This means that a final handful of high-rise condo towers will likely be built on the south side of Wilshire, where the shade test is less of a factor, and likely will command top prices.

By one calculation, the most valuable Westwood land, foot for foot, lies just off the boulevard, unseen by Wilshire travelers. Westwood Memorial Park occupies three acres wedged between the Avco Center high-rise, Westwood Presbyterian Church and the backyards of homes on Wellworth Avenue. The only access is by a Glendon Avenue driveway that doubles as the exit for a parking garage. The cemetery, a city Historic-Cultural Monument that dates to the failed nineteenth-century town of Sunset, rises out of obscurity every August 5, the anniversary of the 1962 death of its most famous occupant, Marilyn Monroe. Her tomb, crypt number 24 in the Corridor of Memories, draws attention and visitors from all over the world.

Tourists who come to see Marilyn discover an almost endless roster of familiar names. Among the passed-on actors and actresses interred are Burt Lancaster, Dean Martin, Natalie Wood and Jack Lemmon. Leading Hollywood figures from behind the camera include *Sunset Blvd.* director Billy Wilder, studio mogul Darryl F. Zanuck and agent Irving Lazar. Famous names from the world of music include songwriter Sammy Cahn, cellist Gregor Piatigorsky, Carl Wilson of the Beach Boys and Roy Orbison. *Playboy's* Hugh Hefner reportedly reserved a crypt next to Monroe—he wanted to lay in rest above her, but that spot was already taken.

CHAPTER NINE

WEST TO THE PACIFIC

WILSHIRE BOULEVARD reveals tasty bits of its past on almost every block. The morsels are shared in the subtle details of street art and architecture, or in the backstory behind an important corner or a vanished landmark. No length of the Grand Concourse evokes a more live, tangible sense of history's sweep than the four miles that arrive, finally, at the inviting blue crescent of Santa Monica Bay. Right there on the ocean bluffs is where horse wagons first rolled along a town street that would get the Wilshire name. That was in 1875, before transcontinental trains or electric lights had reached frontier Los Angeles, and two decades ahead of Gaylord Wilshire's real estate dalliance in a barley field beside Westlake Park.

A curious visitor who knows what to listen for might be lucky enough to imagine the clomp of a

Eucalyptus windbreaks had grown in at the ocean end of Nevada Avenue by the time Gaylord Wilshire turned his first spade of earth fourteen miles inland. In the distance, a horse-drawn wagon moves along the only rails to be laid along the future boulevard.

thousand worn army boots, the mournful wail of a bugle or the rasp of a steamship's whistle. The final leg begins where Westwood's office towers stop, at the intersection of Wilshire and Veteran Avenue. The busy corner ranks near the top of the most traversed crossings in contemporary Los Angeles, but it used to be the end of the line. Blocking the way seaward for travelers from the city were the farms and orchards of a picturesque federal preserve that in its heyday drew tourists from all over.

The Pacific Branch of the National Home for Disabled Volunteer Soldiers and Sailors opened in 1888, eleven difficult miles west of Los Angeles but only a short distance inland from the coastal village of Santa Monica. Civil War veterans came there to live out their years "commanding a fine view, sheltered from winds of the north by mountains and open to the ocean breezes." Soldiers' Home, as the newspapers short-handed it, housed as many as five thousand men in a rambling colony of Victorian barracks surrounded by gardens, fields and wild ravines that streamed out of the mountains.

Remnants of the original Soldiers' Home are still visible along Wilshire Boulevard. Closest to Westwood, and the most dramatic reminder, is Los

Disabled veterans of the Civil War and Indian skirmishes filled the 1888 Soldiers' Home and tended the grounds. Wilshire Boulevard would later cross right to left in the foreground.

Angeles National Cemetery, where eighty-seven thousand American warriors and their loved ones are commemorated on 114 acres. It started as a small Boot Hill, donated by rancho holder John Wolfskill, after "a gray-haired soldier named Prather failed to answer 'adsum' to his name" at roll call, the *Times* reported in May 1889. Abner Prather had been a Union blue in the 4th Indiana Infantry before finding his way to the plain west of Los Angeles. His original wood-plank marker near the undulating cemetery's highest point has been upgraded to a marble gravestone, just one of the countless that file in emotion-tugging ranks under century-old trees. The cemetery's presence is not well-appreciated by Angelenos, but the solemn grounds have stood in for Arlington National Cemetery in numerous films and television episodes.

Near Prather's secluded grave, a simple yet elegant granite obelisk honors soldiers who fought in the Spanish-American War, the foray inspired by publisher William Randolph Hearst, egged on by Harrison Gray Otis and fought by Teddy Roosevelt, among others. Elsewhere lie fourteen recipients of the Congressional Medal of Honor, their service spanning from the Korea Campaign of 1871 to World War II.

Each Memorial Day, Soldiers' Home members dressed in fraying uniforms to pay their respects. Staff members of the home, wives and children were eligible for burial and their original grave markers still stand in a corner of the Los Angeles National Cemetery.

Memorial Day at Cemetery, Soldiers' Home, Cal.

Buried nearby are also more than one hundred Buffalo Soldiers, the African Americans who first fought in the Indian Wars of the American frontier, plus veterans of the Chinese Boxer Rebellion and all the conflicts of the twentieth century through the Vietnam War. Two loyal dogs, Blackout and Old Bonus, have received national burials there. In *The Black Echo,* a novel by Edgar Award-winner Michael Connelly, FBI agent E.D. Wish can't stand that her office, up high in the federal office building across Wilshire, faces such a gallant collection. "All those graves," she sighs. "I try never to look out the windows there."

Some of the men buried there had marched hundreds of miles to apply for membership in the Soldiers' Home. Private George Davis, of the 14th New York Cavalry, arrived first on May 2, 1888. Soon, a thousand men were camped around him, awaiting the home's opening. It was built on rancho land donated mostly by U.S. Senator John Percival Jones and grew into the largest and most appealing rest spot for old soldiers in the West. Broad manicured avenues curved among evergreen trees and flower gardens. Members,

as they were called, lived in group "domiciliaries" designed in stick-and-shingle style by the architecture firm of Peters and Burns, with attractive verandas overlooking the grounds.

Members tended the orchards and grew lima beans, vegetables and oats for the kitchen. They also kept livestock and a menagerie of other animals, some for eating and some as pets, among them a kangaroo and a cougar. Biologists at California State University Los Angeles say that Southern California can thank the Soldiers' Home men for the aggressive, greenish-coated fox squirrels that roam backyards and parks. They were brought from the Midwest and South by veterans, got loose and quickly spread, driving out the region's more docile native gray squirrels.

At the center of Soldiers' Home life stood a massive three-story dining hall with seating for a thousand. On Memorial Day and for ceremonies, members put on their uniforms and fell into formation outside under the dining hall clock. When one of their own died, a procession would march behind the caisson over to the cemetery. The prospect of catch-

The Chapel, National Soldier's Home, Cal.

Hospital Building, Soldier's Home, Cal.

ing sight of so many white-bearded men in uniform attracted tourists on the Balloon Route that circled from Los Angeles to the coast and back. Trains would pull into the home and stop outside the dining hall, allowing time for photographs with the old soldiers. President William J. McKinley, a former Union officer, paid his respects on May 9, 1901, during the Los Angeles visit where he stayed overnight with General Otis on Wilshire Boulevard. Pictures show throngs of men in suits and bushy mustaches massed in front of the dining hall to hear the president assure the veterans, "That government for which you fought, to which you gave the best years of your lives . . . will see to it that in your declining years you shall not suffer but shall be surrounded with all the comforts and all the blessings which a grateful nation can provide." Four months later, McKinley was assassinated in Buffalo, New York, by an anarchist.

The last original structure—and the oldest located anywhere along Wilshire Boulevard—stood just across the parade grounds when McKinley visited. Construction began in 1899 on a clapboard chapel that architect Charles W. Moore has called "a building with exceptional verve." The westernmost Wilshire entry on the National Register of Historic Places, it was designed by J. Lee Burton as a rare place of worship that houses Protestant and Catholic sanctuaries under the same roof. Divided by a double-brick wall, each side had its own entrance. The Protestant side, consecrated on March 11, 1900, is more Romanesque in motif, while the Catholic half, dedicated a week later, shows Gothic influences. The exterior was originally stained redwood, but the chapel facing Wilshire Boulevard now has been painted a cream color. A wood-framed streetcar depot from the same era and designer also survives not far away; both are closed to the public and in poor repair.

The main Soldiers' Home entry gates, which also remain, faced south toward the town of Sawtelle, founded in 1896. The two places went together. Sawtelle's streets were named for Civil War battle sites (today's Stoner Avenue was Vicksburg, Colby Avenue was Gettysburg) and for the states from which the men hailed. Oregon Avenue, the main route through town, became Santa Monica Boulevard. Town and soldiers developed the kind of mutually beneficial relationship often found around military posts. When the *Times* checked on Sawtelle in 1904, the reporter found three gambling halls (two of them run by veterans) and a house of prostitution. Pension days, when the men got paid in cash, were especially tawdry occasions. As much as eighty thousand dollars would be

Memorial Day Review,
Soldier's Home, Cal.

Newspapers covered the Soldiers' Home like a small town, reporting on social affairs, notable arrivals and departures, and the crop yield. Suicides were not infrequent, sometimes right on the cemetery grounds. The 1900 double-opening of the Catholic and Protestant chapels, far left, was big news. Ceremonies were commonly held outside the dining hall, often in view of tourists.

dispensed each month, "and with wolfish eagerness, a horde of thugs, gamblers, prostitutes and sellers of evil liquors lay in wait . . . at the very gates of the Soldiers' Home," the paper reported. Men often staggered back to the grounds drunk and robbed of their money after sprees in Sawtelle's taverns.

The town also became somewhat renowned as the best place in the West for women of a certain age to find a husband. There was never a shortage of lonely men with guaranteed pensions seeking companionship. Sawtelle recorded more marriages involving a spouse over sixty than anywhere in the country, the *Times* reported in 1917, and at one wedding more than thirty grandchildren attended. Even after they married, the men could remain Soldiers'

Home members and take meals in the dining room, but they would live in town. One of Sawtelle's most profitable jobs was building small cottages for the new couples. The flip side, naturally, was that over time many widows were left behind. They would receive twelve dollars a month in survivor benefits and could apply for assistance from the Ladies of the Grand Army of the Republic, which raised enough money to erect a "widow's row" of cottages a half-mile west of the home on the lane that ran down to the ocean bluffs in Santa Monica. The lane, Nevada Avenue, became Wilshire Boulevard.

All of it—the Soldiers' Home, Sawtelle, Nevada Avenue and Santa Monica—existed due to the hubris of Senator Jones. He was an English-born Ohioan who reached Southern California via a circuitous path. His family had settled in Cleveland in 1830, when he was a year old. News of the 1848 gold

Members who married typically moved outside the gates into the town of Sawtelle. A "widow's row" of cottages for women who outlived their old soldiers extended west on what became Wilshire Boulevard.

strikes put him in a ship sailing around Cape Horn to San Francisco. Jones apparently never struck it rich in gold, but he did serve as sheriff in remote Trinity County, then won election to the state senate. After losing a bid for lieutenant governor, Jones crossed to Nevada and ran a Comstock Lode silver mine where he made serious money. In 1872 Nevada's legislature sent Jones to the U.S. Senate. He kept the position for thirty years, although he lived for much of that time beside the Pacific, far from the rough-and-tumble mining towns he represented.

Jones had his own boomtown to nourish. He had established Santa Monica as an unlikely seaport on the former *Rancho San Vicente,* a spread of more than thirty thousand acres with lineage traced back to a decree by the king of Spain. Colonel Robert S. Baker, for whom the town of Bakersfield is named, paid fifty-five thousand dollars for the land in 1872. Two years later, Jones took majority control, with Baker—and later his widow, Arcadia Bandini Stearns Baker—as minority partner. By then, a wharf called Shoo Fly Landing served ships steaming past. Tar from the La Brea pits ten miles inland was hauled to the pier in wagons and loaded on freighters bound for San Francisco.

Up the beach about a mile, on the adjacent *Rancho Boca de Santa Monica,* small hotels accommodated vacationers who rode their horses to the edge of the surf to relax at the mouth of Santa Monica Canyon. "A week at the beach will add ten years to your life," one of the inns advertised. Bathhouses soon opened on the beach, pumping ocean water into porcelain tubs where one could soak in private. Jones and his partners, however, had bigger plans. They wanted to make Santa Monica a real town, with a deep-water port for the Los Angeles and Independence Railroad they intended to build to haul silver ore from the Owens Valley, two hundred fifty miles inland. Santa Monica would be their personal blow against the hegemony of the hated Southern Pacific, which viciously controlled shipping in California. When the S.P. would not carry their construction materials, Jones and company brought supplies in by sea and employed Chinese workers to build the railroad from the beach inland toward Los Angeles.

First, though, Jones had to entice people to live in Santa Monica. He mapped out a town with a central square seven blocks back from the coastal bluffs, framed between main streets named for his dual loyalties—Nevada and California. Ocean Avenue ran along the fragile palisades that regularly sloughed off onto the beach below. The morning of the town's opening, July 15, 1875, livery stables in Los Angeles emptied out and the wagon roads to the sea filled with the curious. Steamships delivered potential buyers from San Francisco. Prospects were seated facing the Pacific, as if to be lulled with the loveliness of it all. Free beer flowed. Jones sold forty thousand dollars in lots the first day and made a similar catch the next day. By the end of the year, more than a hundred homes and stores had been completed and Jones's railroad reached Los Angeles.

The senator and his wife took the town's most scenic corner, where Nevada Avenue ended at the ocean cliffs, and erected a lavish three-story mansion, the Miramar, with bountiful gardens and an inviting porch that faced the sunset. South along the bluff about a mile, a grand seaside resort hotel—named the Arcadia, for Mrs. Baker—opened in 1887, the year of the land boom. Its steep gables and soaring cupola stood so tall on the horizon that people back in Los Angeles could see the hotel's outline.

Socialites from the city, among them Gaylord Wilshire, came out and entertained in the Arcadia's ornate rooms. A gravity-driven roller coaster ferried visitors across a nettlesome arroyo that separated the hotel from the settled portion of town.

Santa Monica also became a weekend beach getaway. Trains brought revelers from Los Angeles to play in the bathhouses and clubs that opened on the beachfront below the Arcadia and in a dozen saloons. The action became too raucous for some tastes. Newspapers railed about cardsharps and shell-game runners and called for marshals to police the trains for indecent acts and the "lawlessness of the Los Angeles hoodlums, male and female." Frederick Rindge, who lived on Nevada Avenue near Jones and for years would reign over the *Rancho Topanga Malibu Sequit* up the coast, persuaded the town trustees in 1890 to close the saloons; they soon reopened as restaurants where purveying alcohol was legal again.

Santa Monica's popularity as a resort averted an early demise. The town's brief spell as a port had ended abruptly when Jones sold his fledgling railroad to the Southern Pacific, which had ruthlessly undercut him by slashing fares. The S.P. promptly shut down the railroad and the wharf at Santa Monica. In the 1890s, the Southern Pacific's new president Collis P. Huntington revived the idea of a seaport at Santa Monica. He built an astonishing wharf north of Santa Monica Canyon that curved forty-three hundred feet out from shore to reach deep water. Huntington felt his Port Los Angeles would ensure the Southern Pacific's dominance, since all cargo passing through would have to pay the railroad's fares. It worked for a short time. More than seven hundred fifty ships called at Santa Monica between 1893 and 1896. But the venture ultimately

failed when Los Angeles interests, led by *Times* publisher Harrison Gray Otis, persuaded the U.S. Congress to endorse construction of a "free port" at San Pedro. Stripped of its importance, Santa Monica's so-called Long Wharf fell into disuse and became a fishing pier and tourist curiosity before being torn down in the early 1920s.

JONES STITCHED TOGETHER his big-picture real estate strategy like a master. In the Senate, he lobbied hard for the Soldiers' Home to be placed on his land, over a rival location in San Bernardino. It was just good business. The home delivered an infusion of government money in the form of construction funds, salaries and pensions to the Santa Monica area. He also provided the land for Sawtelle. A horse-drawn streetcar on Nevada Avenue shuttled Soldiers' Home denizens to and from Santa Monica.

Nevada Avenue, finally renamed Wilshire Boulevard in 1913 in shrewd anticipation of a future link to Los Angeles, connected all the elements of Jones's creation. From the start, big things happened there. The first game of golf in Southern California was played on a polo field at Nevada and Seventh Street, a "perfectly flat plain of hard-beaten mud, plentifully strewn with coins and shreds of barks from the surrounding eucalyptus trees, but without a single blade of grass." Nevada Avenue took on a certain grandeur under the care of Abbot Kinney, a colorful figure in the annals of Santa Monica and Los Angeles. He is best-known as the creator of the quirky Venice canals, the pride of a large resort development called Venice-by-the-Sea. Kinney was also a California Club brother of Gaylord Wilshire and they were alike in some ways. Both men traveled the

Racers called the hard left onto Nevada Avenue a "dead man's curve" even though no lives were lost there until 1916. By then, Ocean Avenue was paved and the boulevard was called Wilshire. Cars carried a driver and a mechanic with tools.

world and hardly fit the mold of mainstream city builders. Kinney had studied in France, toured Europe on foot, and after selling his share of the family's cigarette brand for a small fortune sailed for Egypt. He arrived in California "as a developed specimen: well traveled, well read, well languaged," historian Kevin Starr wrote.

One of Kinney's causes became the breeding and planting of Australian eucalyptus trees as windbreaks and landscape features. He served as chairman of the state board of forestry and, during a stint as local road commissioner, planted a grove of his beloved gum trees on both sides of Nevada Avenue. In his leisure pursuit as a top tennis player, Kinney helped build a club at Third Street and Washington

Avenue, giving Santa Monica a formative new upscale image. Members included Gaylord Wilshire and Senator Jones, but the club's prestige flowed from the tennis champions Santa Monica produced. Marion Jones, the senator's daughter, won the U.S. Open in 1899 and 1902. Elizabeth "Bunny" Ryan won in doubles at England's venerated Wimbledon competition nineteen times, after young May Sutton showed the way. One of four tennis-playing Sutton sisters from Santa Monica, May began taking local tournaments at age twelve, won the U.S. Open champion at age sixteen, and at eighteen became Wimbledon's first American champion. In 1911, Sutton married another local tennis star, Thomas Clark Bundy. They were the It Couple of Santa Monica society, the Bay City's

U.S. Senator John P. Jones of Nevada built the Miramar as his country home in 1888-89. It overlooked Santa Monica Bay from the end of the future Wilshire Boulevard. His wife is credited with planting a Moreton Bay fig tree that has become a city historic landmark.

Pickford and Fairbanks. Their home on 25th Street, built in 1913, is a city historic landmark. Considered a savvy real estate player, Bundy had paid eighteen thousand dollars for the northeast corner of Wilshire and La Brea and sold it in the 1920s for four hundred twenty thousand dollars.

Tennis projected a glamorous image, but Santa Monica became better known as the home of immensely popular automobile road races. In July 1909, the first major grand prix-style race held in Southern California attracted fifty thousand spectators. They stood along Nevada Avenue and other streets, where the dirt had been smoothed and oiled to cut down the flying dust, to cheer the most famous drivers of the day. Racers began in front of a grandstand at

Ocean and Montana avenues, veered left onto Nevada around Dead Man's Curve, then sped counter-clockwise over an 8.4-mile course. The route included a three-mile straightaway east on Nevada, then a wide left turn through the Soldiers' Home and a dash back to the coast along what became San Vicente Boulevard through the new residential subdivisions of Westgate and Brentwood Park. At the first race, a veteran named W.W. Swain watched a car roar by then fell over dead. Too much excitement, the newspapers blared.

Photos of chain-driven roadsters tearing past palm trees in winter served as good advertising for the automobile companies and promoted Santa Monica to frigid Easterners as a sunny idyll, wrote author Harold Osmer in his book *Real Road Racing.* Competition stopped for World War I, then resumed for a final run in 1919. By then Santa Monica had grown, many streets were paved, and residents no longer felt safe with speedsters careening through the community. The following year racing moved onto the new wood speedway track on Wilshire Boulevard in Beverly Hills. Santa Monica was ready to move into the future.

Two years before his Ambassador Hotel opened in Los Angeles, architect Myron Hunt designed a hulking 368-room hotel to rise twelve stories from the beach where Wilshire Boulevard ends at the coast. Luckily for future beholders of the ocean view, the monstrosity never got built. The following year, in 1920, Parkinson and Parkinson were asked to draw plans for remodeling the late Senator Jones's Miramar estate into a hotel. His home did function as a hotel for

After Jones died, his mansion was converted into a hotel also called the Miramar. In the 1920s, designs were considered for mammoth beachfront hotels that would soar above the ocean bluffs at the terminus of Wilshire. None of them were built.

By 1922 Abbot Kinney's eucalyptus trees along Wilshire had grown tall. Pilots at the new Douglas factory and airfield on the eastern edge of Santa Monica took care to avoid them.

awhile; eventually, the mansion was removed and an ocean-view tower built, with private bungalows around the property. "Where Wilshire meets the sea . . . warmer in winter, cooler in summer," the Hotel Miramar advertised. A rangy Moreton Bay fig tree on the front entry drive, said to have been planted in 1889 by Mrs. Jones, enjoys city landmark status.

The Miramar lacked the panache of the Ambassador or the Beverly Wilshire, but it gave the coastal end of Wilshire Boulevard a signature establishment. Wilshire from the beach back to the Soldiers' Home still clung to its country-lane charm, but changes were coming. In the early 1920s, aviation innovator Donald Douglas moved his airplane factory into a vacated movie studio lot on the north side of Wilshire at 25th Street. A short dirt and grass airstrip could handle small craft, so long as they avoided the thick line of eucalyptus trees that marked the path of Wilshire Boulevard. Larger planes had to be rolled through the streets to Santa Monica's Clover Field, which had a longer runway. After Douglas moved its factory across town to the municipal field (and in World War II became Santa Monica's largest employer), the last pilot to take off from Wilshire Boulevard in 1927 was reportedly Charles Lindbergh.

Airplanes left Wilshire just in time. Newly paved through the Soldiers' Home in 1928, the boulevard finally reached all the way from the Pacific inland to Westlake Park, via Westwood, Beverly Hills and the Miracle Mile. Abbot Kinney's double row of eucalyptus trees was sacrificed to widen the boulevard, some of the timber used to build an attractive guard rail along the ocean bluffs. Wilshire's passage through Santa Monica never evolved into another Miracle Mile, but it turned into a flourishing business street. The Spanish Colonial Revival-style Lindke building at Fourth Street opened in 1925. At Seventh, the Wilshire Professional Building gave the Santa Monica stretch a modern Art Deco office tower similar to those farther east, but on a smaller scale.

Also at Seventh Street, the land originally set aside by Jones for a town square was developed into the lovely Lincoln Park, with the St. Monica parish church standing at the California Avenue end. In the park, the Miles Memorial Playhouse, designed in 1926 by John Byers, draws praise from architecture critics Gebhard and Winter as "one of the boulevard's most significant public structures . . . a gracefully sober rendering of the Spanish Colonial Revival." The Wilshire Theater near Fourteenth Street brought a further taste of Art Deco to the boulevard.

The city of Sawtelle ceased to exist after residents accepted annexation into Los Angeles in 1922. By the end of the decade, many street names had been changed and the area became officially part of West Los Angeles. Warren G. Harding High School was renamed University High; just off Wilshire Boulevard, an artesian spring on the campus is believed to be a former *Gabrieleño* Indian site where the Spanish-led Portolá expedition camped in 1769. The Sawtelle label survives only on a narrow avenue that defines a small community of mostly Japanese–American shops and nurseries and passes former hotels and rooming houses before entering the former Soldiers' Home grounds.

The home itself added the large Wadsworth Hospital in 1927, and three years later the entire reservation became part of the new federal Veterans Administration. Hoover barracks were built during the Depression to house the homeless, but after World War II the last of the wooden nineteenth-century domiciliaries were razed as fire hazards, and the facility's role as a residence gradually changed. The remaining five hundred acres and one hundred forty buildings belong mostly now to the Department of Veterans Affairs West Los Angeles Healthcare Center, and as the last large open parcel on the Westside, there is pressure to sell off prime frontage along Wilshire Boulevard for commercial development. If that is attempted, however, descendants of Jones and Baker might make a fuss. The rancho land was donated in the 1880s for the perpetual benefit of veterans.

WILSHIRE BOULEVARD'S final westward run, three downhill miles from the ex-Soldiers' Home to the statue of St. Monica at the ocean, provides a suitable finish to the Grand Concourse. It's not beautiful, but it is a flourishing stretch of medium-rise office complexes that house ad agencies, the newsrooms of *People* magazine and *Entertainment Weekly,* and the consulates of Great Britain, Switzerland, Italy and New Zealand. At street level, a hundred restaurants and coffee purveyors, plus supermarkets, drive-up pharmacies, car showrooms, a post office and a hospital, claim every inch of sidewalk.

An overhead installation of public art celebrates the border between Los Angeles and Santa Monica, and with it Wilshire Boulevard's arrival at the bay. The ceremonial steel arch at Franklin Street, by artist Tony DeLapp, is the only structure to span the width of Wilshire other than the San Diego Freeway. It

curves forty-two feet above the pavement with a playful jog near the peak, a flourish meant to symbolize an ocean wave. Crossing under The Wave, the streetscape turns perceptibly more upscale. Santa Monica treats Wilshire Boulevard with more honor than does Los Angeles, providing a landscaped median and a young generation of palm trees. In Santa Monica, Wilshire is a Tropic of Affluence that separates the quieter, more affluent upper side of town from the more crowded business latitudes to the south.

The old Douglas airfield has become an attractive public park with a pond and stream. Closer to the ocean, Lincoln Park—site of the first makeshift game of golf in 1897—has been re-christened Christine Emerson Reed Park, in memory of a former mayor. The boulevard brushes past the head of Third Street Promenade, a wildly successful reinvention of a faded strip mall into an urban walking village. It has become what some wish Westwood Village could be again, a thriving center of shopping, restaurants and movie theaters.

Santa Monica's Wilshire Theatre debuted at Euclid Street late in 1930, "rushed to completion in record time" during an era when new cinemas were opening in several places along the boulevard.

At Ocean Avenue, Wilshire reaches the end of the run with a pair of serviceable architectural ornaments, neither of which delivers the excitement demanded by the exquisite edge-of-the-Pacific locale. At the corner where Senator Jones built his mansion, the latest incarnation of the Miramar is a pricey Fairmont hotel. The entrance driveway circles under the impressive cantilever canopy of Mrs. Jones's mature Moreton Bay fig. Across the intersection at 100 Wilshire, the lowest address found anywhere on the boulevard, a white Streamline Moderne office tower spikes twenty-one stories into the sky. The tallest structure in Santa Monica, the Cesar Pelli design (built for television bandleader Lawrence Welk) is not unattractive and surely is more pleasing to look at than the One Wilshire hulk at the opposite end of the boulevard. Yet it fails to elevate the terminus where Wilshire ends—or where the Grand Concourse begins, depending on one's historical preference.

A more delightful closure can be found across Ocean Avenue in Palisades Park, behind the folded arms and beatific glance of St. Monica. Looking across the sparkling bay on a clear day, distant Catalina Island surfaces in the blue on the left, beyond the point of Palos Verdes. Curving to the right are Malibu and Point Dume. Below the bluffs is the last surviving Santa Monica Pier, not the great seaport that Senator Jones envisioned, but a world-famous tourist destination with a historic carousel and arcades. Jones used to walk over and sit on the same bluff opposite his mansion to receive the sunset in the 1890s. A memorial plaque marks the spot.

If they could come back, Gaylord Wilshire and any of the boulevard creators who followed him— Henry O'Melveny, A.W. Ross, Mary Pickford, Arthur Letts, among many others—would surely be amazed. Wilshire Boulevard's exalted status in the cultural zeitgeist of Los Angeles is secure, even though its service as a linear downtown proved to be a "transitional rather than definitive urban form," urban planner Doug Suisman wrote. With the growth of mini-downtowns scattered across the city, Wilshire Boulevard's role changed. It surely fell short of some less realistic expectations; it never became a West Coast Champs-Elysees or Fifth Avenue, for example. Instead, Wilshire is something more daring and unique, the embodiment of the motorized dreams and optimistic reach for the future that invented Los Angeles. The metropolis could not have arisen anywhere else, and Wilshire Boulevard was the accidental, but necessary, creation that let the future begin. "The living mirror of contemporary Los Angeles in all its manifestations," architecture critic Leon Whiteson once wrote. "To know Los

Ground at Seventh Street was broken in 1928 for the Santa Monica Professional Building, described as Spanish Colonial Revival with Plateresque details. Developers there agreed with their Los Angeles counterparts that distinctive architecture would pay off on the boulevard.

Angeles, you need to know Wilshire Boulevard."

If there is an irritating flaw in the legacy, it is that Wilshire Boulevard lacks the one signature icon, the unmistakable skyline symbol, that shouts "Los Angeles" the way the Transamerica pyramid proclaims San Francisco or the Chrysler and Empire State buildings are icons for New York. Frank Gehry, the architect whose Santa Monica home sits two blocks off the boulevard, told an interviewer that his breathtaking steel Walt Disney Concert Hall in downtown Los Angeles belongs on Wilshire, where the people are. He suggested it would fit nicely next to the Wadsworth Theater, a performance space near the historic chapel on the old Soldiers' Home grounds. Certainly, the Museum of Contemporary Art would engage more with the city on Wilshire's Museum Row than it does on Bunker Hill downtown. Or imagine the spectacular Getty Center museum down on Wilshire, amid the city instead of perched on a hard-

to-reach ridge, isolated from any temptation to just drop in. On Wilshire the Getty would have become a focal point of city street life, the way New York's Metropolitan Museum is on Fifth Avenue.

Wilshire, though, does not demand an uplifting symbol to hold its special place in the city's lore. The boulevard's reign gathers new respect all the time. Stylish neon street signs announce the old Wilshire Center and Miracle Mile districts. The relighting of rooftop neon displays along the boulevard, many of them switched off for half a century after World War II, has been called by Kevin Starr, "one of the most imaginative and cost-effective redevelopment schemes in Los Angeles history." At night, when the beacon twinkles atop the Bullock's

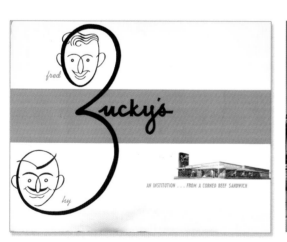

WILSHIRE MOTEL
12023 Wilshire Blvd. (Midway between Santa Monica & Westwood)
Los Angeles 25, California

Stephen's Motor Hotel - 11955 Wilshire Blvd. West Los Angeles 25, Cal.

Wilshire's final four miles down to the Pacific has been a mishmash of retail businesses. Nearly all of the motels and service stations have disappeared, along with restaurants such as Zucky's and Bob Burns' that were beloved community landmarks. Madame Wu's Garden at Wilshire and 22nd Street had a private room for celebrity diners such as Frank Sinatra.

Wilshire tower and the colorful rooftop tubes advertise the Bryson, the Park Wilshire and the Gaylord, no other Los Angeles boulevard comes close to matching Wilshire's classic magic.

Photographs of the early boulevard are being displayed proudly in more places along the route—in the pool lobby of the Beverly Wilshire Hotel, behind the counter of an optometrist's office on the Miracle Mile, in the nearby International House of Pancakes, on the walls of the Starbucks at the Fox Theater in Westwood. An art installation inside the Crest Theater on Westwood Boulevard offers an homage to the long-vanished Carthay Circle Theater, which most of the Crest's patrons never saw. The Carthay Circle is also memorialized in a street scene a long way from home, at the Disney–MGM Studios in Orlando, Florida. Universal Studios Florida has a copy of the Brown Derby hat and a movie-lot miniature of the Beverly Wilshire Hotel façade. Wilshire's past, it would seem, forms an essential part of the Los Angeles image everywhere.

Its attractions have endured through changing tastes and the slippage of time. Jack Smith, the late *Los Angeles Times* columnist and an unabashed fan, urged his readers to eschew the freeways and navigate Wilshire just for the joy of it. Wrote Smith, "Wilshire Boulevard at night, in its deceptive slumber, is Los Angeles at its finest." Simply, it's the Grand Concourse of history and dreams for the city that loves to drive.

St. Monica, patroness of the city, receives Wilshire Boulevard's arrival at the bay with beatific serenity. The statue in Palisades Park was commissioned in 1934 by the federal Public Works of Art Project and sculpted by Eugene Morahan.

ACKNOWLEDGMENTS

THIS BOOK BENEFITS from the earlier work and boundless generosity of many historians, photographers, collectors, researchers and fans of Wilshire Boulevard and of Los Angeles. We are grateful to each of them for sharing, and for their inspiring determination to get things right. For their cheerful and illuminating guidance, we wish to thank the staff of the history department of the Los Angeles Public Library, especially photography curator Carolyn Kozo Cole and maps guru Glen Creason. Dace Taube of the Regional History Collection at USC was helpful when we needed it most. Cynni Murphy of the Santa Monica Public Library and everyone at the UCLA Special Collections Library aided tremendously. We enjoyed a stunning level of cooperation from the Los Angeles Conservancy, and give special thanks to Linda Dishman, Ken Bernstein, Cathy Gudis, Anne Laskey, Jane McNamara, Cindy Olnick, Adriene Bondo, Jan Saiget and Shannon Simmons.

We treasure the suggestions and research insight provided by Alan Hess, John English, Margaret Tante Burke, Steven Sann, Lisa Landworth, Sally Landworth, Philip J. Debolske, Anne Salenger, Patty Lombard, Kay Balue and Charles Perry. For the use of their photographs and images, we offer the most heartfelt thanks to Tom Zimmerman, Ernest Marquez, Julius Shulman and Judy McKee, Jim Heimann, Chris Nichols, Nathan Marsak, Bob Reiss, Anne Laskey, and Russ Mason at Clear Channel Outdoor. We are grateful for the assistance of Julie Silliman and Pat Gomez of the City of Los Angeles Cultural Affairs Department, Tom Breckner of the Los Angeles Department of Recreation and Parks, Linda Whisman of Southwestern University School of Law, Jim Walker of the Dorothy Peyton Gray Transportation Library, Linda Harris Mehr of the Margaret Herrick Library at the Academy of Motion Picture Arts and Sciences, and Gary Kurutz and Vickie Lockhart of the California State Library.

Carla Lazzareschi earned our respect and gratitude for deftly nurturing this project for much of its life. The book also benefitted greatly from the work of her colleagues Linda Estrin and Michael Diehl. The Los Angeles Times graciously allowed us use of the photographs and news clippings maintained by the editorial library, and we thank all of the librarians there and directors Cary Schneider and Dorothy Ingebretsen for letting us get in the way on many late nights. This is our first collaboration with Angel City Press, and we would like to express our delight at getting to know and work with Paddy Calistro, Scott McAuley, Amy Inouye and Jacqueline Green. Special thanks go to Kathy McGuire and Lindsay Hagans for their thoughtful improvements to the manuscript.

Kevin would also like to congratulate Judy Graeme and Sean Roderick for making it to the end, and thank them for their love and support. Eric thanks the friends he walked Wilshire Boulevard with many years ago and who inspired his interest in doing a book: Matthew Pearson, Daniel Fogg, Dennis Miles and especially Phil McKinley.

BIBLIOGRAPHY

NOTE

The Wilshire Family Papers located at UCLA provided original material about Gaylord Wilshire and his boulevard. The book is also based on City of Los Angeles records, Los Angeles Conservancy files, historical maps and documents, contemporary accounts in the *Los Angeles Times* and other newspapers, and interviews conducted by the author or researcher. Their understanding of the boulevard's importance benefitted greatly from scholarly works by many historians, especially Thomas Hines, Kevin Starr, Richard Longstreth, William Deverell, Greg Hise and Tom Sitton.

PUBLISHED SOURCES

- Banham, Reyner. *Los Angeles: The Architecture of Four Ecologies.* London: Penguin Press, 1971.
- Beasley, Delilah L. *The Negro Trail Blazers of California.* New York: Negro Universities Press, 1919.
- Bengtson, John. *Silent Echoes: Discovering Early Hollywood Through the Films of Buster Keaton.* Santa Monica: Santa Monica Press, 2000.
- Berger, Robert. *Sacred Spaces: Historic Houses of Worship in the City of Angels.* Glendale: Balcony Press, 2003.
- *The Blue Book & Club Directory 1925.* Los Angeles: Bulfer & Hoag, 1925.
- Bottles, Scott L. *Los Angeles and the Automobile: The Making of the Modern City.* Berkeley: University of California, 1987.
- *The Brown Derby Cookbook.* Garden City: Doubleday, 1949.
- Burk, Margaret Tante. *Are the Stars Out Tonight?* Los Angeles: Round Table West, 1980.
- Carr, Harry. *Los Angeles, City of Dreams.* New York: Grosset & Dunlap, 1935.
- Caughey, John and LaRee. *Los Angeles: Biography of a City.* Berkeley: University of California, 1976.
- Chew, Robert Z. and David D. Pavoni. *Golf in Hollywood.* Santa Monica: Angel City Press, 1998.
- Cigliano, Jan and Sarah Bradford Landau, eds. *The Grand American Avenue, 1850-1920.* San Francisco: Pomegranate Artbooks, 1994.

- Clary, William W. *O'Melveny and Myers, 1885-1965.* Los Angeles: privately printed, 1966.
- Cleland, Robert Glass. *California in Our Time (1900-1940).* New York: Alfred A. Knopf, 1947.
- Clover, Samuel T. *A Pioneer Heritage.* Los Angeles: Saturday Night Publishing, 1932.
- Cobb, Sally Wright and Mark Willems. *The Brown Derby Restaurant.* New York: Rizzoli, 1996.
- Davis, Margaret Leslie. *Bullocks Wilshire.* Los Angeles: Balcony Press, 1996.
- Davis, Mike. *Ecology of Fear.* New York: Metropolitan, 1998.
- Ford, John Anson. *Thirty Explosive Years in Los Angeles County.* San Marino: The Huntington Library, 1961.
- Frick, Devon Thomas. *I. Magnin & Co.: A California Legacy.* Garden Grove: Park Place Press, 2000.
- Fulton, William: *The Reluctant Metropolis: The Politics of Urban Growth in Los Angeles.* Baltimore: Johns Hopkins University Press, 1997.
- Gebhard, David and Robert Winter. *Architecture in Los Angeles: A Compleat Guide.* Salt Lake City: Gibbs Smith, 1985. Revised as *An Architectural Guidebook to Los Angeles,* 2003.
- ——, ed. *Myron Hunt, 1868-1952: The Search for a Regional Architecture.* Santa Monica: Hennessey & Ingalls, 1984.
- —— and Harriette von Bretton. *Los Angeles in the Thirties: 1931-1941.* Los Angeles: Hennessey & Ingalls, 1989.
- Gottlieb, Robert and Irene Wolt. *Thinking Big: The Story of the Los Angeles Times, its Publishers, and their Influence on Southern California.* New York: GP Putnam, 1977.
- Graves, J.A. *My Seventy Years in California.* Los Angeles: The Times-Mirror Press, 1927.
- Greenstein, Paul and Nigey Lennon, Lionel Rolfe. *Bread and Hyacinths: The Rise and Fall of Utopian Los Angeles.* Los Angeles: California Classics, 1992.
- Gudis, Catherine: *Buyways: Billboards, Automobiles and the American Landscape.* Routledge (New York) 2004.
- Guiles, Fred Laurence. *Marion Davies.* New York: McGraw-Hill, 1972.

- Guinn, J.M. *A History of California and an Extended History of Los Angeles and Environs.* Los Angeles: Historic Record Co., 1915.
- Hancock, Ralph. *Fabulous Boulevard.* New York: Funk & Wagnalls, 1949.
- Heimann, Jim. *California Crazy and Beyond: Roadside Vernacular Architecture.* San Francisco: Chronicle Books, 2001.
- ——. *Car Hops and Curb Service: A History of the American Drive-in Restaurant, 1920-1960.* San Francisco: Chronicle Books, 1996.
- ——. *Out With the Stars: Hollywood Nightlife in the Golden Era.* New York: Cross River Press, 1985.
- Herr, Jeffrey, ed. *Landmark L.A.: Historic–Cultural Monuments of Los Angeles.* Santa Monica: City of Los Angeles Cultural Affairs Dept. / Angel City Press, 2002.
- Hess, Alan. *Googie: Fifties Coffee Shop Architecture.* San Francisco: Chronicle Books, 1985.
- Hines, Thomas. "The Linear City: Wilshire Boulevard, Los Angeles 1895-1945," chapter in *The Grand American Avenue, 1850-1920,* Jan Cigliano and Sarah Bradford Landau, eds.
- Hise, Greg and Deverell, William. *Eden by Design: The 1930 Olmsted-Bartholomew Plan for the Los Angeles Region.* Berkeley: University of California, 2000.
- *Historical Record & Souvenir, Los Angeles County Pioneer Society.* Los Angeles: Times Mirror Press, 1923.
- Historic Resources Group. "Wadsworth Chapel Historic Structure Report." Historic Resources Group, 2001.
- Hudson, Karen E. *Paul R. Williams, Architect: A Legacy of Style.* New York: Rizzoli, 1993.
- Hunt, William Dudley. *Total Design: Architecture of Welton Becket and Associates.* New York: McGraw-Hill, 1972.
- Keane, James Thomas. *Fritz B. Burns and the Development of Los Angeles.* Los Angeles: Loyola Marymount, 2001.
- Kilner, William H. B. *Arthur Letts, a Biography.* Los Angeles: Young & McCallister 1927.
- Kimball, Byron. *Street Names of Los Angeles.* Los Angeles: Los Angeles Bureau of Engineering, 1988.

- Longstreth, Richard. *City Center to Regional Mall: Architecture, the Automobile, and Retailing in Los Angeles, 1920-1950.* Cambridge: The MIT Press, 1997.
- ——. *The Drive-in, the Supermarket, and the Transformation of Commercial Space in Los Angeles, 1914-1941.* Cambridge: The MIT Press, 1999.
- *Los Angeles City Directory.* Los Angeles: Los Angeles Directory Co., various years.
- Ludwig, Carolyn. *Jewels in Our Crown: Churches of Los Angeles.* Los Angeles: Ludwig, 2003.
- Luther, Mark Lee. *The Boosters.* Indianapolis: Bobbs-Merrill, 1923.
- Marquez, Ernest. *Santa Monica Beach: A Collector's Pictorial History.* Santa Monica: Angel City Press, 2004.
- McCoy, Esther. *Five California Architects.* Los Angeles: Hennessey & Ingalls, 1987.
- McDougal, Dennis. *Privileged Son.* Cambridge: Perseus, 2001.
- McGrew, Patrick and Robert Julian. *Landmarks of Los Angeles.* New York: Harry N. Abrams, 1994.
- Moore, Charles et al. *The City Observed: Los Angeles.* New York: Vintage Books, 1984.
- Nadeau, Remi. *City-Makers.* Corona del Mar: Trans-Anglo Books, 1977.
- Naylor, David. *Great American Movie Theaters.* Washington: Preservation Press, 1987.
- Newmark, Maurice and Marco R., eds. *Sixty Years in Southern California, 1853-1913.* Los Angeles: Dawson's Book Shop, 1984.
- Nichols, Chris ed. "Built By Becket." Los Angeles Conservancy Modern Committee, 2003.
- Olmsted, Frederick Law and Harland Bartholomew, Charles Henry Cheney. "A Major Traffic Street Plan for Los Angeles." Committee on Los Angeles Plan of Major Highways of the Traffic Commission of the city and county of Los Angeles, 1924.
- Osmer, Harold and Phil Harms. *Real Road Racing: The Santa Monica Road Races.* Chatsworth: Harold Osmer, 1999.

- ——. *Where They Raced: Auto Racing Venues in Southern California, 1900-1920.* Chatsworth: Harold Osmer, 2000.
- Pitt, Leonard and Dale Pitt. *Los Angeles A to Z.* Berkeley: University of California, 1997.
- Quint, Howard H. *The Forging of American Socialism: Origins of the Modern Movement.* Columbia: University of South Carolina, 1953.
- Sitton, Tom. *John Randolph Haynes: California Progressive.* Stanford: Stanford University Press, 1992.
- —— and William Deverell, eds. *Metropolis in the Making: Los Angeles in the 1920s.* Berkeley: University of California, 2001.
- Smith, Jack. *Jack Smith's L.A.* New York: McGraw-Hill, 1980.
- Spalding, William A. *History and Reminiscences, Los Angeles City and County, California.* Los Angeles: J.R. Finnell & Sons, 1931.
- Starr, Kevin. *Inventing the Dream: California through the Progressive Era.* New York: Oxford University Press, 1985.
- ——. *Material Dreams: Southern California through the 1920s.* New York: Oxford University Press, 1990.
- Suisman, Douglas R. *Los Angeles Boulevard: Eight X-rays of the Body Public.* Los Angeles: Los Angeles Forum for Architecture and Urban Design, 1989.
- Sutton, Horace. *The Beverly Wilshire Hotel.* Beverly Hills: Regent Beverly Wilshire, 1989.
- Thomas de la Pena, Carolyn. *The Body Electric: How Strange Machines Built the Modern American.* New York: New York University, 2003.
- Thorpe, Edward. *Chandlertown: The Los Angeles of Philip Marlowe.* New York: St. Martin's Press, 1983.
- Tygiel, Jules. *The Great Los Angeles Swindle: Oil Stocks and Scandal During the Roaring Twenties.* New York: Oxford University Press, 1994.
- Valentine, Maggie. *The Show Starts on the Sidewalk: an Architectural History of the Movie Theatre, Starring S. Charles Lee.* New Haven: Yale, 1994.

- Van Tuyle, Bert. *Know Your Los Angeles: An Unusual Guidebook.* Los Angeles: H.E. Ahlrich, 1940.
- Wallace, David. *Lost Hollywood.* New York: St. Martin's Press, 2001.
- Warren, Charles S., ed. *Santa Monica Community Book.* Santa Monica: Arthur W. Cawston, 1944.
- Weddle, David. *Among the Mansions of Eden: Tales of Love, Lust and Land in Beverly Hills.* New York: William Morrow, 2003.
- Welty, Earl M. and Frank J. Taylor. *The Black Bonanza.* New York: McGraw-Hill, 1956.
- *Who's Who Among the Women of California.* San Francisco: Security Publishing, 1922.
- *Who's Who in Los Angeles 1925–26.* Los Angeles: Who's Who in Los Angeles Publishers, 1926.
- Wilshire, Gaylord. *Wilshire Editorials.* New York: Wilshire Book Co., 1906.
- Wilshire, Logan. Untitled biography of Gaylord Wilshire, unpublished. Manuscript in Wilshire Family Papers, Charles E. Young Research Library Department of Special Collections at the University of California, Los Angeles.
- "Windows of Immanuel." Los Angeles: Immanuel Presbyterian Church, 1975.
- Workman, Boyle. *The City That Grew.* Los Angeles: The Southland Publishing Co., 1936.

These magazines and journals also provided valuable material: *American City, Artland, ArtScene, Architectural Digest, Hygeia, Land of Sunshine, Liberty, Los Angeles, Los Angeles Saturday Night, Pacific Coast Architect, Pacific Historical Review, Parks and Recreation, Southern California Quarterly, Southwest Builder and Contractor, Touring Topics, UCLA Magazine, Uptown Wilshire, Western Architect and Engineer, Western City, Westways* and *Wilshire's Magazine.*

PHOTOGRAPHY CREDITS

This book includes photographs made available by the *Los Angeles Times* and from other archives and collectors.

When the name of a *Los Angeles Times* staff photographer is known, it is indicated in square brackets. Others, whose names do not appear in the *Times* archives, deserve equal credit.

Los Angeles Times: cover, 1, 2-3, 10, 12, 17, 18, 22-23, 38, 39 (top), 39 (bottom), 42, 46-47 [E.J. Spencer], 47, 49, 51 (left), 51 (right) [Larry Sharkey], 52-53, 54, 59, 65, 73 [Rick Meyer], 81 (left), 84, 93, 94 (bottom) [Lori Shepler], 95, 100-101, 102, 104-105 [Bruce Cox], 106-107, 108, 108, 108, 109 (bottom), 112, 114, 116 (right), 117, 122 (right), 123, 128, 131, 133, 135, 135, 136 (bottom), 138, 139, 144-145, 149, 151, 152-153, 153, 156, 159, 162, 166, 169, 174-175, 176, 177 (right), 178, 179, 180, 180, 181 [Larry Bessel], 190, 198

Photographs not from the *Times* appear on the following pages, courtesy of and thanks to the sources:
- California History Room, California State Library, Sacramento, California: 70, 71, 72, 74, 82-83, 89, 164-165
- Clear Channel Communications: 102-103, 115
- Jim Heimann: 41, 62 (right), 64 (right), 97 (left), 120-121, 154-155, 157
- Alan Hess: 182
- Anne Laskey: 107 (top), 127 (right)
- Los Angeles Public Library, *Herald Examiner* Collection: 60
- Los Angeles Public Library, Security Pacific Collection: 11, 30-31, 34, 35-36, 56 (bottom), 62 (left), 68-69, 78-79, 111, 116 (left), 122 (left), 125, 134, 141, 167, 175, 177 (left), 189
- J. Eric Lynxwiler: 8 (left), 13, 20, 25, 29, 32-33, 40, 50, 55, 56 (inset), 57, 58, 61, 77, 81 (right), 86, 94 (top), 97 (bottom right), 99, 109 (right), 110, 113, 118 (left), 124, 129, 130, 132-133, 137, 142 (left), 155, 160 (bottom), 161 (bottom), 163, 173, 186, 187, 188, 195, 200 (top and bottom right), 201, endpapers
- Ernest Marquez: 6-7, 19, 92, 170, 171, 184-185, 192, 193, 194, 196
- Nathan Marsak: 136 (top), 160 (top), 161 (top)
- Chris Nichols: 1 (top), 64 (left), 97 (top and center right), 118-119 (bottom), 143 (right)
- Bob Reiss: 118 (center), 142 (right), 143 (left), 200 (left)
- Santa Monica Public Library: 199, 200 (center)
- Julius Shulman: 118-119 (center)
- Bruce Torrence: 90-91
- Wilshire Family Papers, UCLA: 14-15, 24, 26
- University of Southern California, on behalf of the USC Specialized Libraries and Archival Collections: 4-5, 8 (right), 9, 88, 126 (top), 147, 148
- Tom Zimmerman: 126-127

INDEX

Looking west on Wilshire from the top
of the Gaylord Hotel circa 1930.

Cover and page 1: Viaduct of Westlake Park, 1937.
Pages 2-3: Miracle Mile, circa 1939.
Pages 4-5: Brown Derby and Ambassador, circa 1940.

Wilshire Boulevard: Grand Concourse of Los Angeles
Copyright © 2005 by Kevin Roderick and J. Eric Lynxwiler

Designed by Amy Inouye, www.futurestudio.com

First edition
10 9 8 7 6 5 4 3 2 1

ISBN-10: 1-883318-55-6 // ISBN-13: 978-1-883318-55-0

Library of Congress Cataloging-in-Publication Data

Roderick, Kevin.
   Wilshire Boulevard : grand concourse of Los Angeles / by Kevin
Roderick ; with research by J. Eric Lynxwiler.-- 1st ed.
      p. cm.
   Summary: "Wilshire Boulevard is the unofficial Main Street of
dreams flowing through Los Angeles history. Like Los Angeles
itself, Wilshire is an accidental phenomenon created out of civic
pride and the yearning of the masses to drive. Its 15-mile route to
the sea has been called the Fifth Avenue of the West and the
Champs Elysees of the Pacific"--Provided by publisher.
   Includes bibliographical references (p.   ) and index.
   ISBN-13: 978-1-883318-55-0 (hardcover : alk. paper)
   1. Wilshire Boulevard (Los Angeles, Calif.)--History.
2. Wilshire Boulevard (Los Angeles, Calif.)--History--Pictorial
works. 3. Los Angeles (Calif.)--History. 4. Los Angeles (Calif.)--
Biography. 5. Los Angeles (Calif.)--Buildings, structures, etc. I.
Lynxwiler, J. Eric, 1973- II. Title.
   F869.L875W55 2005
   979.4'94--dc22

2005019406

Printed in China

ANGEL CITY PRESS
2118 Wilshire Blvd. #880
Santa Monica, California 90403
310.395.9982
www.angelcitypress.com